SHAWNEE POTTERY IN COLOR

by

Dolores H. Simon

Additional copies of this book may be ordered from:

COLLECTOR BOOKS
P.O. Box 3009
Paducah, Kentucky 42001

@$8.95 Add $1.00 for postage and handling.

Prices Revised 1981
ISBN: 0-89145-030-0

Printed by IMAGE GRAPHICS, Paducah, Kentucky

COLLECTOR BOOKS
P. O. BOX 3009
PADUCAH, KENTUCKY 42001

THE HISTORY OF
THE
SHAWNEE POTTERY COMPANY

The Shawnee Pottery Company began operations in 1937 in Zanesville, Ohio, and became yet another of many successful potteries to utilize the abundant natural resources of the Muskingum River Valley region. Until the pottery closed early in 1961, they made a high quality yet inexpensive type of ware that was both novel and functional.

Located at 2200 Linden Avenue, the impressive tri-level buildings of wood, brick and steel construction contained some 500,000 square feet of floor space on thirty acres of grounds with frontage on the Muskingum River. These facilities had previously housed the American Encaustic Tile Company; which as a result of the depression had declared bankruptcy early in the 1930's.

The company title was chosen on recommendation of stockholder Malcolm Schweiker after his discovery of an arrowhead while touring the factory grounds prompted him to delve into the local Indian lore. When investigation revealed that the area had once been dotted by many Indian villages and settlements, he suggested that the firm take for its name that of the tribe of Indians who had inhabited these villages--the Shawnee.

The pottery's early trademark was a Shawnee Indian with an arrowhead. Advertising pieces may be occasionally found with this type of mark; but these are extremely rare, and would be considered a valuable asset to any Shawnee collection.

Addis E. Hull, Jr. came to Shawnee as head of the

company from The Hull Pottery Company of Crooksville, Ohio, a firm founded by his father. Shawnee's success was due in part to the increased feeling of hostility between this country and Germany and Japan. As the supply of imported wares dwindled, our chain stores looked for inland sources to supply them. The principle product of the company from 1937 to 1942 was decorated pottery for the S. S. Kresge Co., S. H. Kress Co., F. W. Woolworth Co., McCrory stores, and Sears and Roebuck and Co. These companies designed their own patterns for such items as flower pots, vases, bowls, dishes, figurines, and jardinieres. George Schwerber modeled the pieces, and Clifford Twiggs made the dies and cases. Next in volume came dinnerware and kitchenware for the Sears and Roebuck Company.

Shawnee's first designer was Rudy Ganz, a German whose fine work for a monument company in Fort Smith, Arkansas prompted Mr. Hull to hire him. He worked for Shawnee from 1939 to 1944, and during that time designed many styles of cookie jars which proved to be very successful for the company. One of the best selling designs was the Smiling Pig -- other popular cookie jars were Jack and Jill, Elephant, Sailor Boy, and Puss N Boots.

Two other early designers were Bouise Bauer, who later worked for the Hull Pottery Company, and Edward Hazel (1942 - 1944).

When Rudy Ganz left the company in 1944, Robert Heckman was recommended by the Ceramics Art Department of Ohio State as his replacement. Mr. Heckman continued as designer for Shawnee for several years.

Several jobbers. . . .among them Great Northern and the Rum Rill Pottery. . . . .designed their own pieces, but did not manufacture them. The Red Wing Pottery Company of Red Wing, Minnesota produced pottery for Rum Rill before 1938, when Shawnee submitted a lower bid and as a result, George Rum Rill awarded the contract to the Shawnee Pottery. Decorative pottery was made for Rum Rill, and later lamps were made for various lamp manufacturers. Special items were made for the premium trade, such as cookie jars, coffee pots, creamers, sugars, and mixing bowls. Their largest premium account was with Proctor and Gamble; however, no records exist today to show the selection of the premium items they once offered.

Addis Hull, Jr. left the Shawnee Pottery Company in March of 1950, and went from there to the Western Stoneware Company in Monmouth, Illinois. He was succeeded by Albert P. Braid as President. That same year, Malcolm Schweiker sold his interest in the company to a syndicate in Philadelphia.

As the market was again becoming flooded with novelty pottery of the type produced at Shawnee, the company suffered great financial loss in 1954. During that year John F. Bonistall came to Shawnee as executive vice-president and general manager. After three months with the company, he was elected president and placed on the board of directors. Under his leadership, many new lines were introduced, and sales greatly increased. He abolished expensive hand decorating and substituted the spray gun method; he himself designed many original pieces in keeping with an Americana theme rather than Oriental or European. His first and most successful line was Touche. For this he used a low-cost paint which turned out an expensive-looking glaze. Other art lines were Liana, Chantilly, Fairy Wood, Petit Point, Fernware, Cameo, and Elegance.

Perhaps the most popular line of all with today's collectors is the Shawnee Corn line. Prior to 1954 this line was called Corn King. When Mr. Bonistall came to Shawnee, however, he changed the glaze to a darker green and re-named it Corn Queen. Although the mark and number remained the same, Corn Queen may be recognized by the darker foliage and lighter kernels.

Shawnee continued to produce a variety of items such as casseroles, lobster sets, console sets, grandaughter clocks, lazy susans and bathroom accessories. Ashtray designs were Monte Carlo, Studio, Flight, Artique, Riviera, and Hostess.

Under the leadership of Mr. Bonistall, Shawnee became one of the largest and most successful pottery in the country. The Dun and Bradstreet (sic?) report of December 31, 1959, showed their net worth to be $895,576. When the pottery closed in 1961, Mr. Bonistall purchased the moulds. He started a ceramics business, Terrace Ceramics, in Marietta, Ohio where he produced a corn line, banks, cookie jars, ashtrays, etc. From there the old Shawnee moulds went to various pottery companies.

SHAWNEE'S METHODS OF PRODUCTION

Abundant clay deposits and a plentiful supply of natural gas in the area, resulted in the establishment of many potteries in the Zanesville, Ohio vicinity--and as a result this city has long been recognized as a great pottery center. Some of the finest examples of art pottery have been produced there.

In ancient times before the development of glaze, primeval tribes coated their pottery with grease, which soaked into the burned ware and made it suitable for use. Application and burning of glaze on clayware gives the surface a vitreous covering to protect the inner body; interior glazing prevents liquids from being absorbed through the porous material. As a general rule, the ware is burned first to make the body; the glaze is applied and the piece burned a second time.

The Shawnee Pottery used a rather unique method of glazing their wares. . . .preferring to fire them only once. As a result, they were able to produce an excellent ware at a lower cost. All ware was thoroughly dried before the glaze was applied. In the production of higher price earthenware, one firing was necessary to bake the body, a second was required to fuse the glaze, and a third if an overglaze was desired. . . .although overglazes were usually confined to very expensive wall tile. Shawnee had some difficulty with their one time firing method; however, they had very little waste. Three processes were originated with the company engineers and ceramists which enabled them to operate at a high level of efficiency. The first was in regard to the preparation of the clay used for the body. The clay was washed to remove lignite, which was a soft combustible mineral ranging from peat to bitumious coal, which sometimes enters the clay deposit in the mining process. If the lignite was not removed, it would burn out in the firing, leaving holes and pitting the ware. The second process had to do with the pottery that was moulded by "jiggering". For this operation, Shawnee engineers developed a large drying oven about 150 feet long. The operation began with two men known as "ballers". They placed a properly sized ball of clay into moulds which were then passed on to two "jiggermen". These men pressed the clay into the sides of the moulds by means of a stick or paddle. The jiggering machine was used only if the interior of the piece was regular or round shaped, and only if the top opening was large enough to allow the paddle to be introduced. The "jiggermen" set the moulds containing the wet clay on a slowly moving belt which passed through the long drying ovens. At the other end a man removed the dried ware from the moulds, and four women were stationed there to inspect the ware and to sponge off any defects or marks. This process continued twenty-four hours a day until the moulds were worn out. Using this procedure, 10,000 pieces of ware were jiggered in an eight-hour shift . . .six times more than with the use of the more conventional methods which required the ware to dry twenty-four hours before firing. During the firing process, the ware at Shawnee passed through a steam heated dryer. The third innovation involved the mechanical means employed in slip moulding. Equipment left from the old American Encaustic Tile Company was altered by Shawnee engineers. A tramway 500 feet long was designed and the moulds were placed on trays suspended by the moving tram which carried them by various employees who filled the moulds. Standard procedure for other potteries required that the moulder carry slip to the mould racks where he filled the moulds by hand. The moulds were made of plaster of paris, a porous substance which absorbs the moisture from the slip. At the same time, it draws the clay to the sides of the mould. When the adhering clay is sufficiently thick, the excess slip is poured out and reused.

The Shawnee Pottery Company made quality merchandise, produced for the market with a fast turn-over. Although it can in no way be compared to the art pottery of the type made in the Zanesville area by Roseville or Weller, it holds a place of its own with today's collectors. Many beautiful and interesting pieces were produced. . . .one of my favorite pieces is the black bull shown on the cover. A large, lovely collection of Shawnee pottery is currently displayed in a museum located at Grove, Oklahoma, called Har-Ber Village. . . . and there are still many pieces of lovely pottery of various types to be found in the Zanesville area.

ACKNOWLEDGEMENTS

I wish to express my thanks to the following people. . some who contributed information--and some who helped me locate pottery for my collection: James Webster, Stillwater, Ok.; Mrs. Robert Smith, Galesburg, Ill.; Sally's Shop, Oak Grove, Mo.; and Norris F. Schneider, Zanesville, Ohio. We especially appreciate the valuable help given to us by Mr. John Bonistall, Shawnee Pottery President, who took time from his busy schedule to assist us and to answer our questions. Mrs. Albert E. Lepper whose husband was employed at Shawnee also took the time to help us, and we thank her very much. Lastly, I want to thank my husband Bob and my children for their patience and assistance.

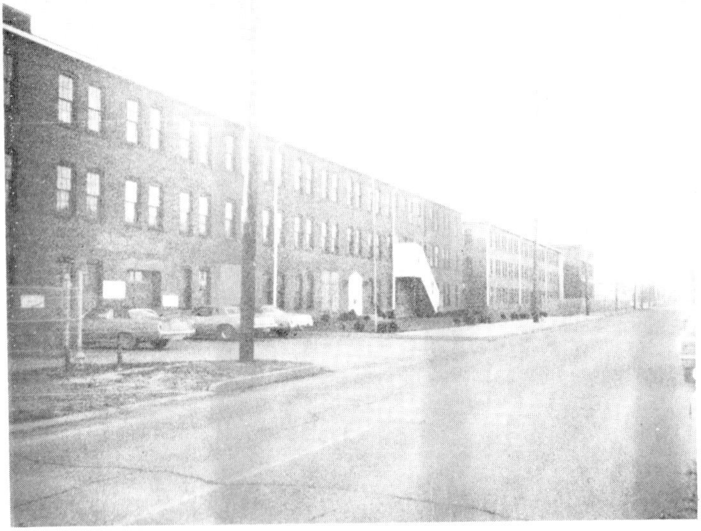

This is a picture of the Shawnee Factory which still stands on Linden Ave., in Zanesville, Ohio. It houses an electrical products company at this time.

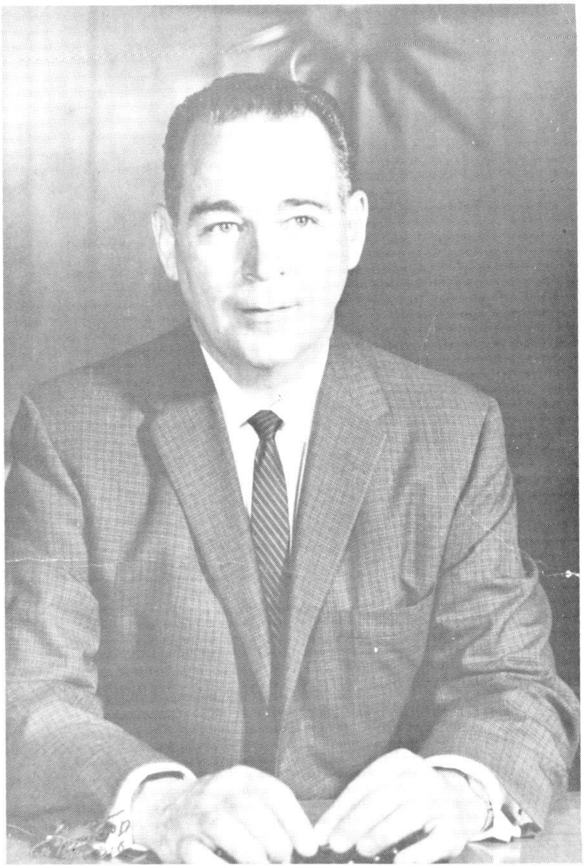

Mr. John F. Bonistall,
President of Shawnee Pottery Company.
(1954 - 1961)

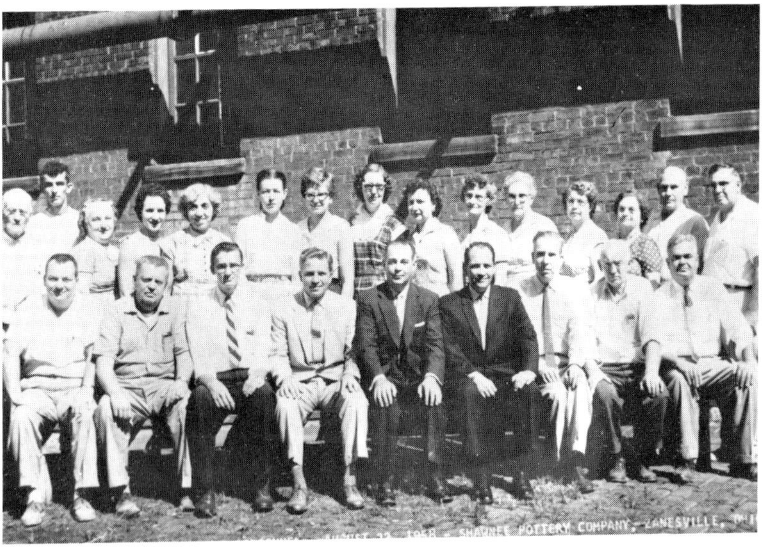

STANDING - Left to Right:

Bill Smith, Kelly Davis, Ted Holsky, Helen Keller, Helen Tracy, Margaret Saad, Irene Everly, Jeanette Shuey, Emily Walker, Pauline Clark, Sylvenia Burkhart, Maude Carpenter, Thelma Fulton, Gertrude Trittipo, Roy Mohr, Bernard Twiggs.

SEATED - Left to Right:

Harris Perkins, A. E. Lepper, Robert Chema, J.C. Shaw, J.F. Bonistall, P.T. Beutell, James Van Sant, Gerald Root, T. H. Abbot

(Not present: James White, Russell Murray, Albert Stemm, Robert Wilson, George Lewis)

Shawnee Pottery

PLATE 1

Top Row - 1. Figural beige ram planter, marked Shawnee U.S.A. # 515; 2. Figural yellow fawn planter, marked U.S.A. # 624, 3. Figural doe and fawn planter, marked U.S.A. #669, 4. Figural deer planter, marked U.S.A. #535.

Middle Row - 1. Figural puppy pushing buggy planter, marked U.S.A. #704, 2. Figural grey and red elephant planter, marked U.S.A. #159, 3. Figural mother goose blue planter, marked U.S.A., 4. Figural yellow duck pulling cart planter, marked Shawnee U.S.A. #752.

Bottom Row - 1. Figural dog lamp, marked U.S.A., 2. Figural elephant planter, marked U.S.A., 3. Figural rocking horse planter, marked Shawnee U.S.A. #660, 4. Figural pekingese and hound planter, marked U.S.A. #611.

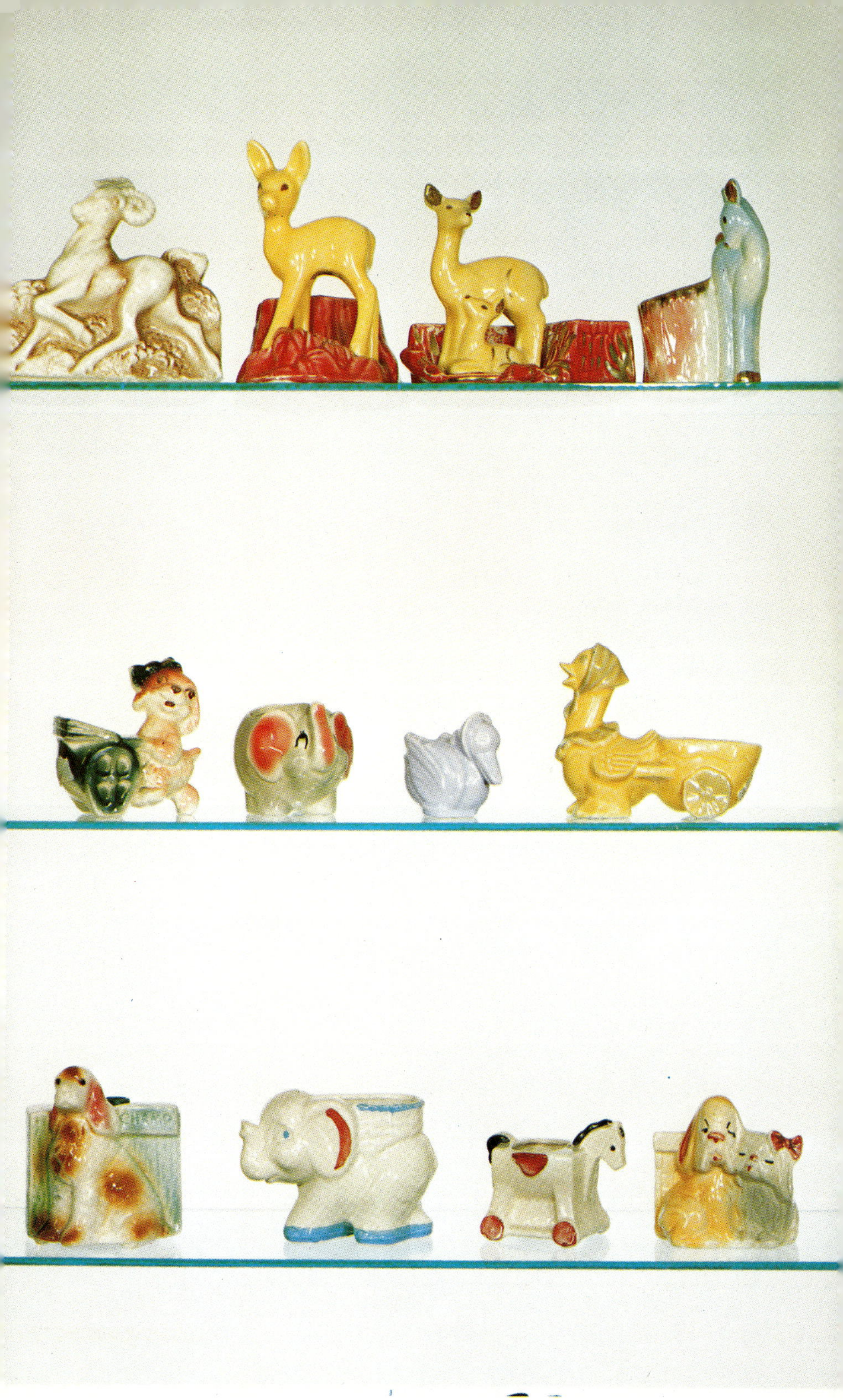
CHAMP

PLATE 2

Top Row - 1. Figural black elephant planter, marked Shawnee U.S.A. 2. Figural black bull planter, marked Shawnee U.S.A. 3. Figural chihuahua in dog house planter, marked Shawnee U.S.A. 4. Figural donkey pulling cart planter, marked U.S.A.

Middle Row - 1. Figural terrier 6" figurine. 2. Figural dog planter, no mark, 3. Figural bloodhound dog planter, marked Shawnee U.S.A. #610, 4. Figural poodle dog riding tricycle planter, marked U.S.A. #712.

Bottom Row - 1. Figural pekingese planter, marked Shawnee U.S.A. 2. Figural donkey planter, marked U.S.A. # 671. 3. Figural birds in birdhouse planter, marked U.S.A. #830, 4. Figural farmer pig with wheelbarrow planter.

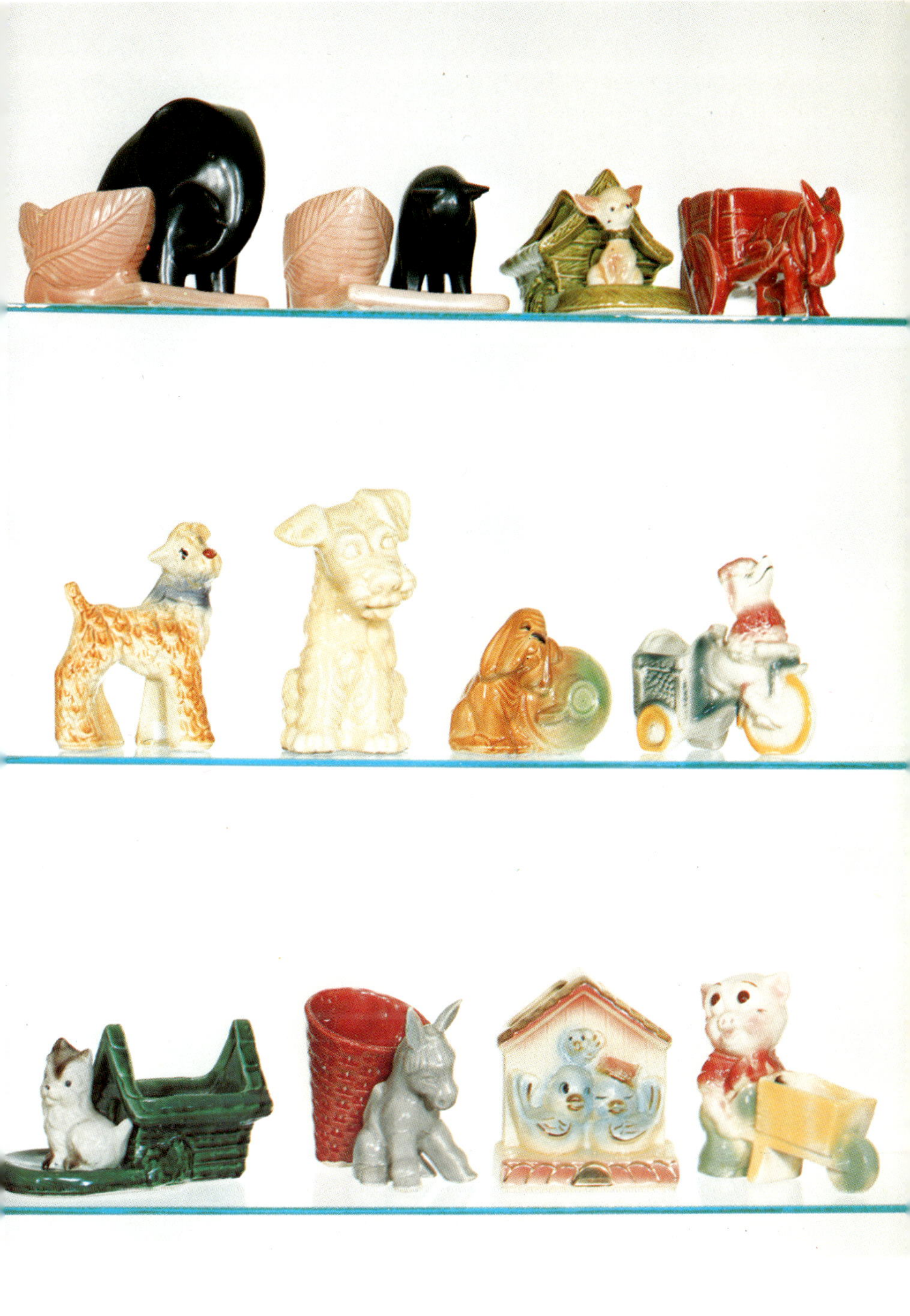

PLATE 3

Top Row - 1. Pair of figural cockatiel planters, marked Shawnee U.S.A. #523, 2. Matching butterfly on bark planter, marked Shawnee U.S.A. #524. 3. Figural geese in rushes planter, marked U.S.A. #707. 4. Rocking horse figural planter, marked U.S.A. #526.

Middle Row - 1. Figural pink horse planter. 2. Figural swan vase marked U.S.A. #806. 3. Figural fish planter marked U.S.A. #717. 4. Figural fawn green caricature vase, marked Shawnee U.S.A. #850. This vase also was made in other colors.

Bottom Row - 1. Pair figural flying geese book ends, marked Shawnee U.S.A. #4000. 2. Figural chick pitcher, marked Patent Pending, 3. Figural gazelle planter, marked U.S.A. #613. 4. Figural pup in shoe planter, marked U.S.A.

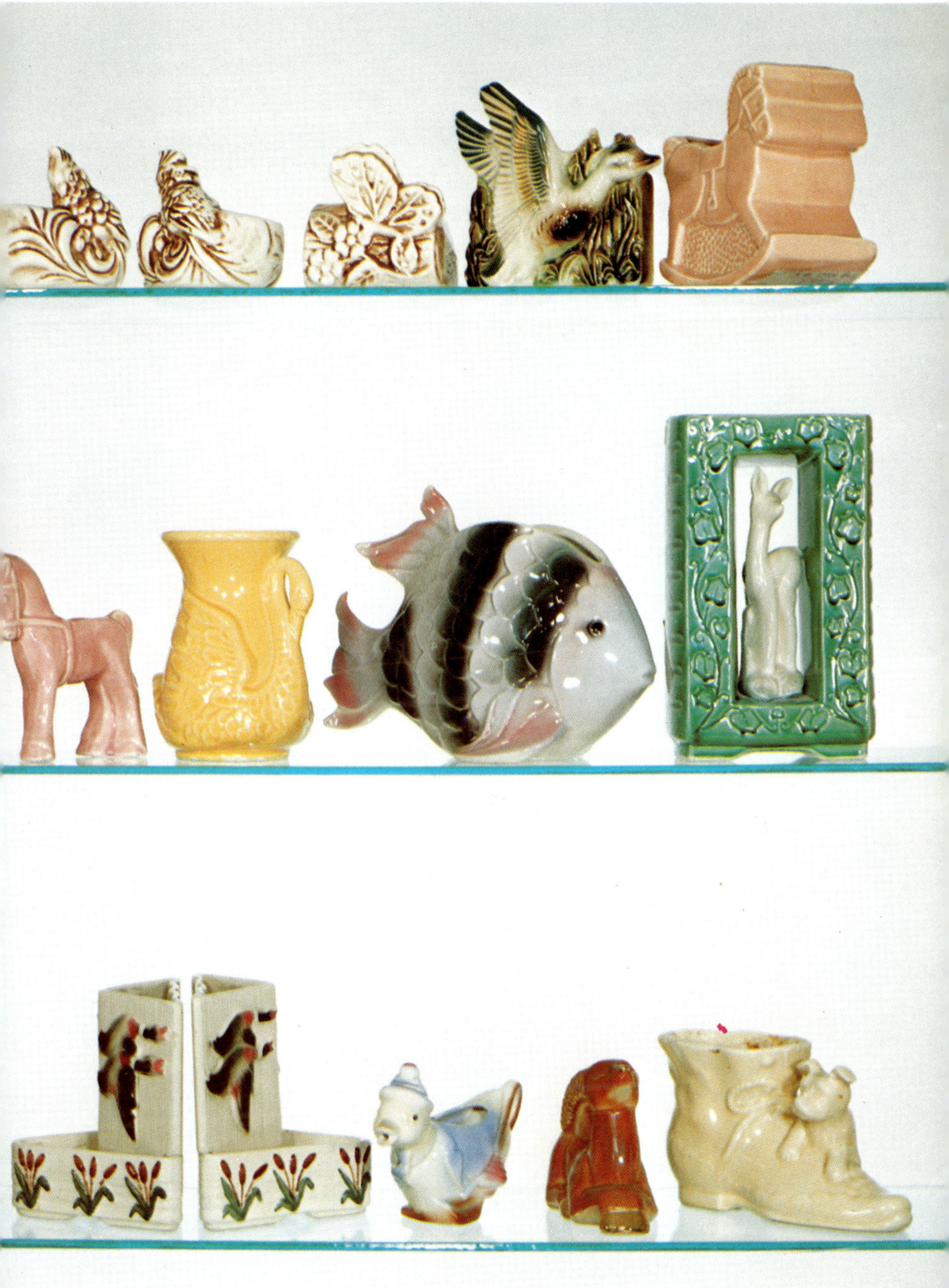

PLATE 4

Top Row - 1. Wishing well planter brown, marked Shawnee U.S.A. #710. 2. Wishing well planter green, marked Swanee U.S.A. #710. 3. Figural elf and shoe planter, marked Shawnee U.S.A. #765. 4. Figural man pushing cart planter, marked U.S.A. #621.

Middle Row - 1. Figural shoe planter, marked U.S.A. #525. 2. Figural boy going fishing planter, marked U.S.A. #532. 3. Figural polynesian lady planter, marked Shawnee U.S.A. #896. 4. Figural boy planter, marked U.S.A. #533.

Bottom Row - 1. Pair oriental people planter, marked U.S.A. #573. 2. Figural girl planter, marked U.S.A. #534. 3. Figural Swiss boy holding duck planter, marked Shawnee U.S.A. #645. 4. Little Jack Horner figural wall vase, marked U.S.A. #585.

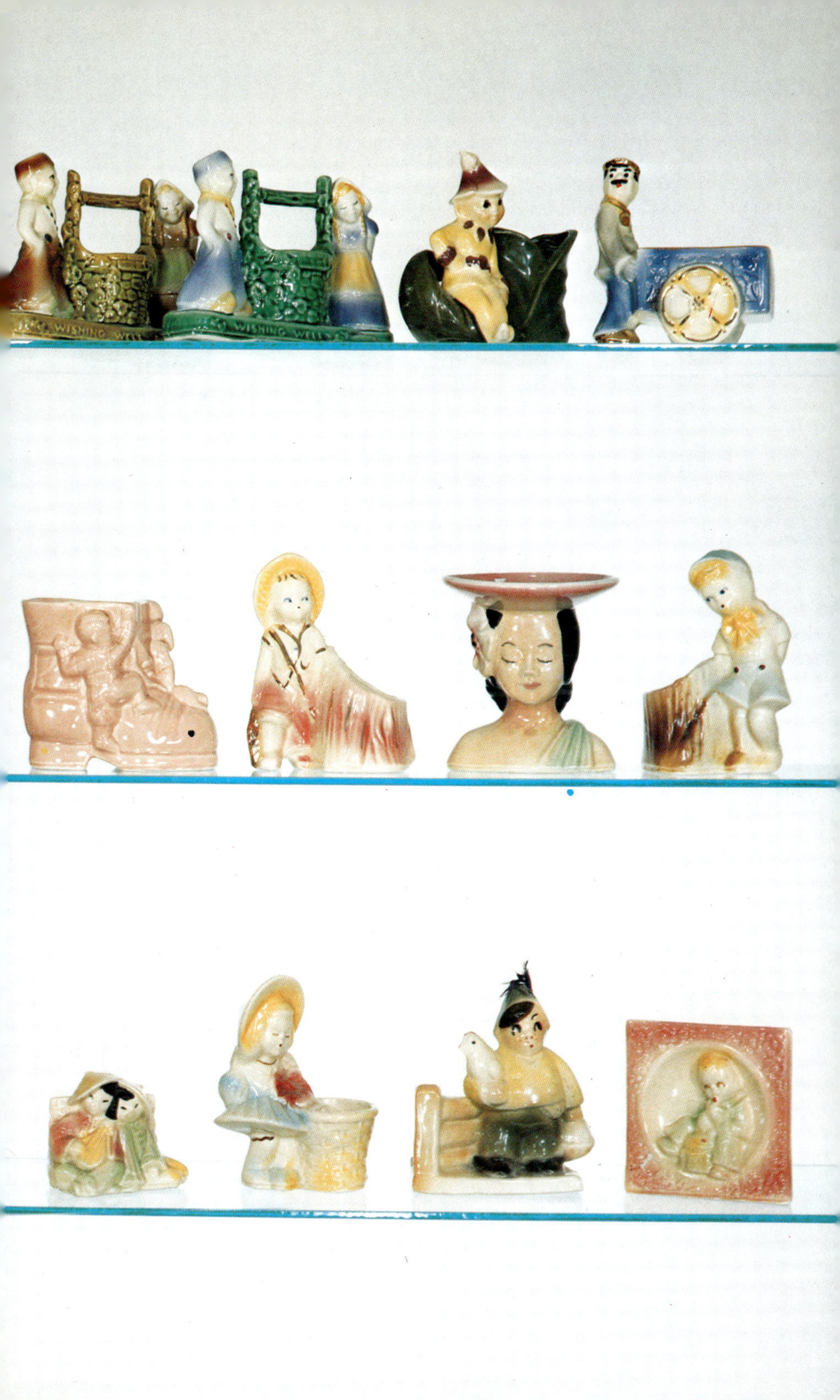
WISHING
WISHING

PLATE 5

Top Row - 1. Pair Swiss children shakers, 2. Pair Dutch children shakers, marked U.S.A. #323. 3. Pair Dutch children same as #2, except have heavy gold overglaze, marked U.S.A. 323S and 323P, 4. Pair Oriental figurines, marked U.S.A. #602.

Middle Row - 1. Oriental girl figurine, marked U.S.A. #601. 2. Same Oriental girl mounted on a planter base, marked U.S.A. #701. 3. Oriental boy planter, marked U.S.A. #702. 4. Figural Chinese man pulling cart planter, marked U.S.A. #539.

Bottom Row - 1. Oriental boy planter, marked U.S.A. #702. This is the same as top row #4 but is mounted on a planter base. Shawnee did this with several of their items. They manufactured pieces in statue form, and used the same designs for planters. 2. Oriental men planter, marked U.S.A. #537. 3. Figural cherub planter, marked Shawnee U.S.A. #536, has original silver and red sticker.

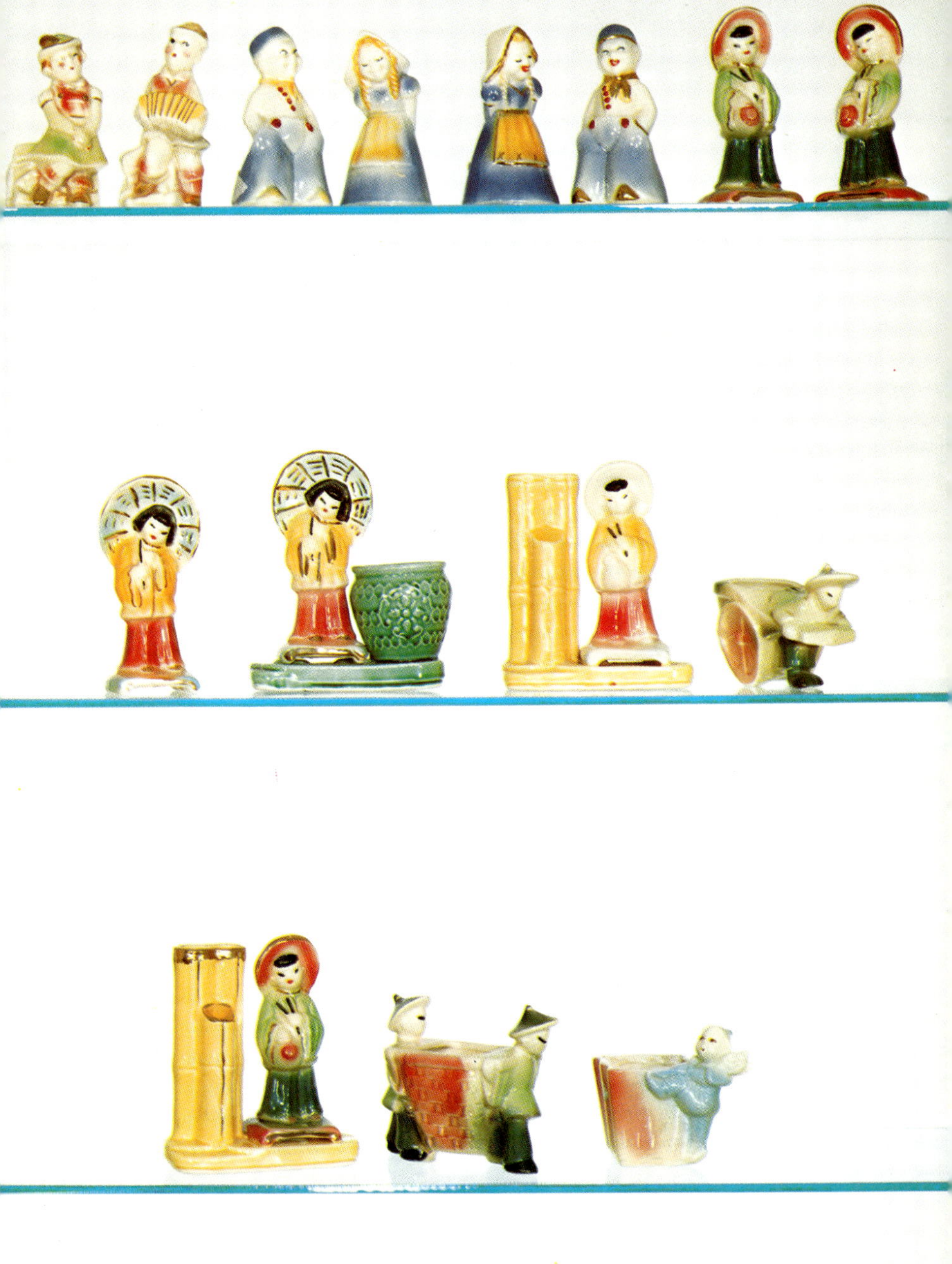

PLATE 6. Corn Line

Top Row - 1. Cookie jar with lid, marked Shawnee U.S.A. #66. 2. Teapot with lid, marked Shawnee U.S.A. #75. 3. Milk pitcher 8½″ tall, marked Shawnee U.S.A. #71.

Middle Row - 1. Mixing bowl, marked Shawnee U.S.A. #5. 2. Individual covered casserole, marked Shawnee U.S.A. ovenproof #73. 3. Platter, marked Shawnee U.S.A. ovenproof #96. 4. Shaker 3½″ tall, no mark. 5. Mixing bowl marked Shawnee U.S.A. #6.

Bottom Row - 1. Pair 5½″ shakers, no mark. 2. Large 11″ covered casserole, marked Shawnee U.S.A. ovenproof #74. 3. Pair of 3½″ shakers, no mark. 4. Oblong relish tray, marked Shawnee U.S.A. #79.

Not pictured - Mixing bowl, same as the two shown only larger and marked Shawnee U.S.A. #8. Individual one cup teapot and lid, much smaller than the one shown, marked Shawnee U.S.A. #65.

Please note the color of the corn kernels on this page and the following page. The lighter kernel with dark foliage is the Corn Queen line and was the newer line. The darker kernels with lighter foliage indicates the older Corn King line.

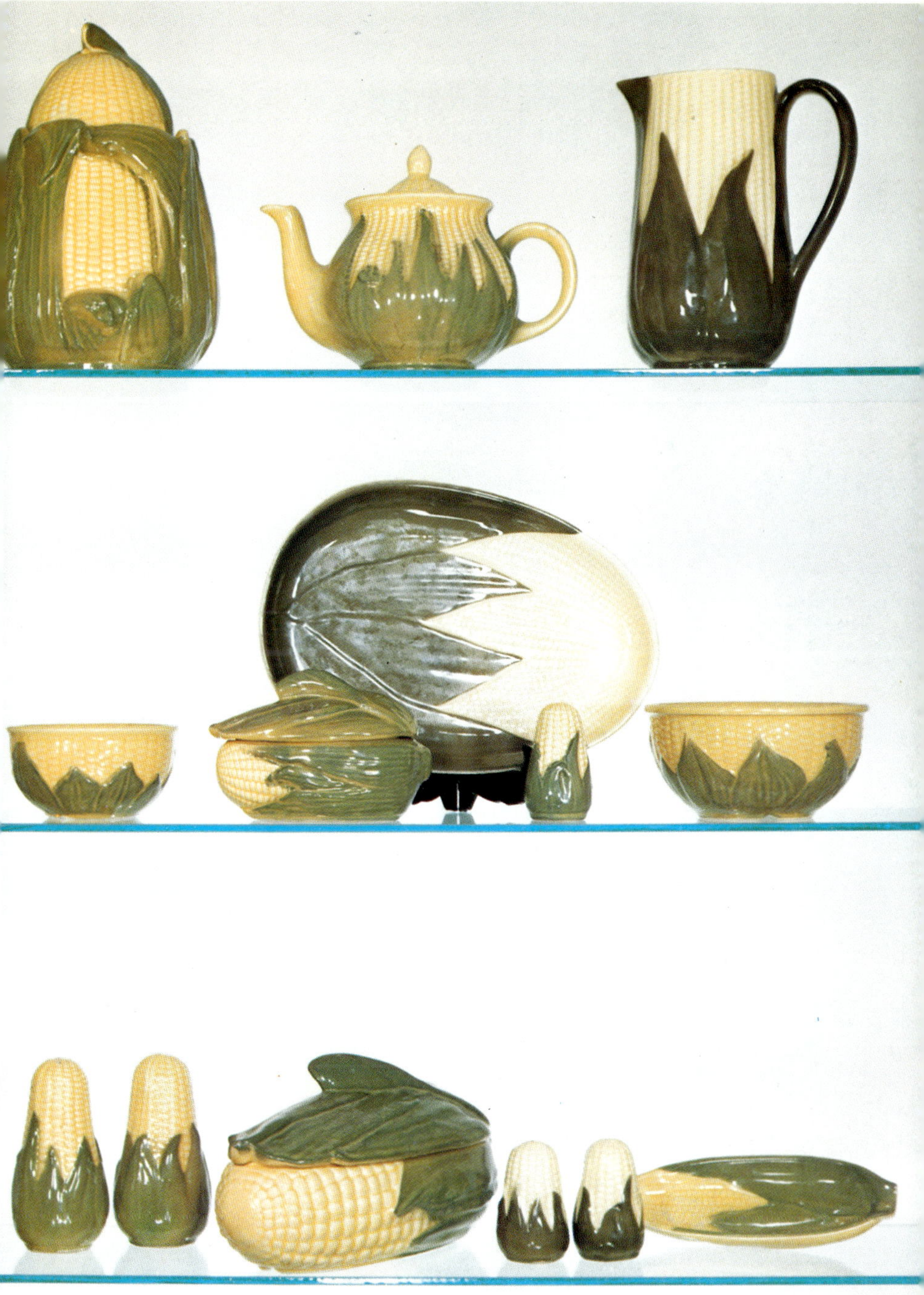

PLATE 7. Corn Line

Top Row - 1. Cream pitcher or syrup pitcher, marked Shawnee U.S.A. #70. 2. Luncheon plate, marked Shawnee U.S.A. #68. 3. Sugar bowl and lid, marked Shawnee U.S.A. #78.

Middle Row - 1. Cereal bowl, marked Shawnee U.S.A. #94. 2. Covered butterdish, marked Shawnee U.S.A. #72. 3. Luncheon plate, marked Shawnee U.S.A. #68.

Bottom Row - 1. Coffee mug, marked Shawnee U.S.A. #69. 2. Dinner plate, marked Shawnee U.S.A. #93. 3. Teacup with saucer, marked Shawnee U.S.A. #90 and #91.

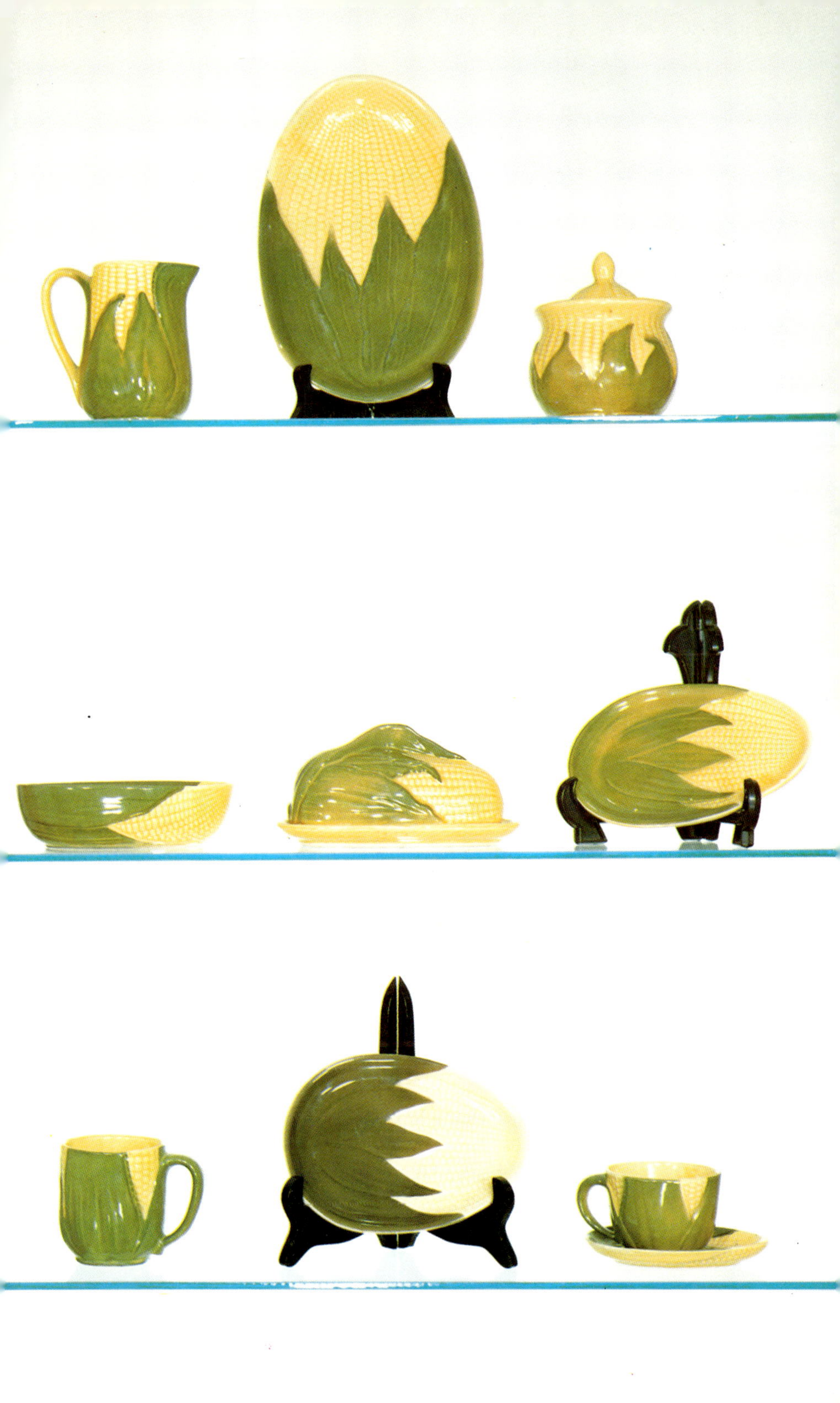

PLATE 8

Top Row - 1. Basket of fruit covered dish, marked Shawnee U.S.A. #81. 2. Cornucopia vase, marked Shawnee U.S.A. #865. 3. Figural dolphin vase, marked Shawnee U.S.A.#828. 4. Basket weave planter, marked Shawnee U.S.A. #444.

Middle Row - 1. Bow Knot double planter, marked Shawnee U.S.A. #518. 2. Figural elephant teapot, marked U.S.A. 3. Figural piano planter, marked Shawnee U.S.A. #528.

Bottom Row - 1. Figural pump planter, marked Shawnee U.S.A. #716. 2. Figural globe planter, marked Shawnee U.S.A. #635. 3. Figural pump lantern, marked Shawnee U.S.A. #716. This one has heavy gold overglaze. Was manufactured in several colors.

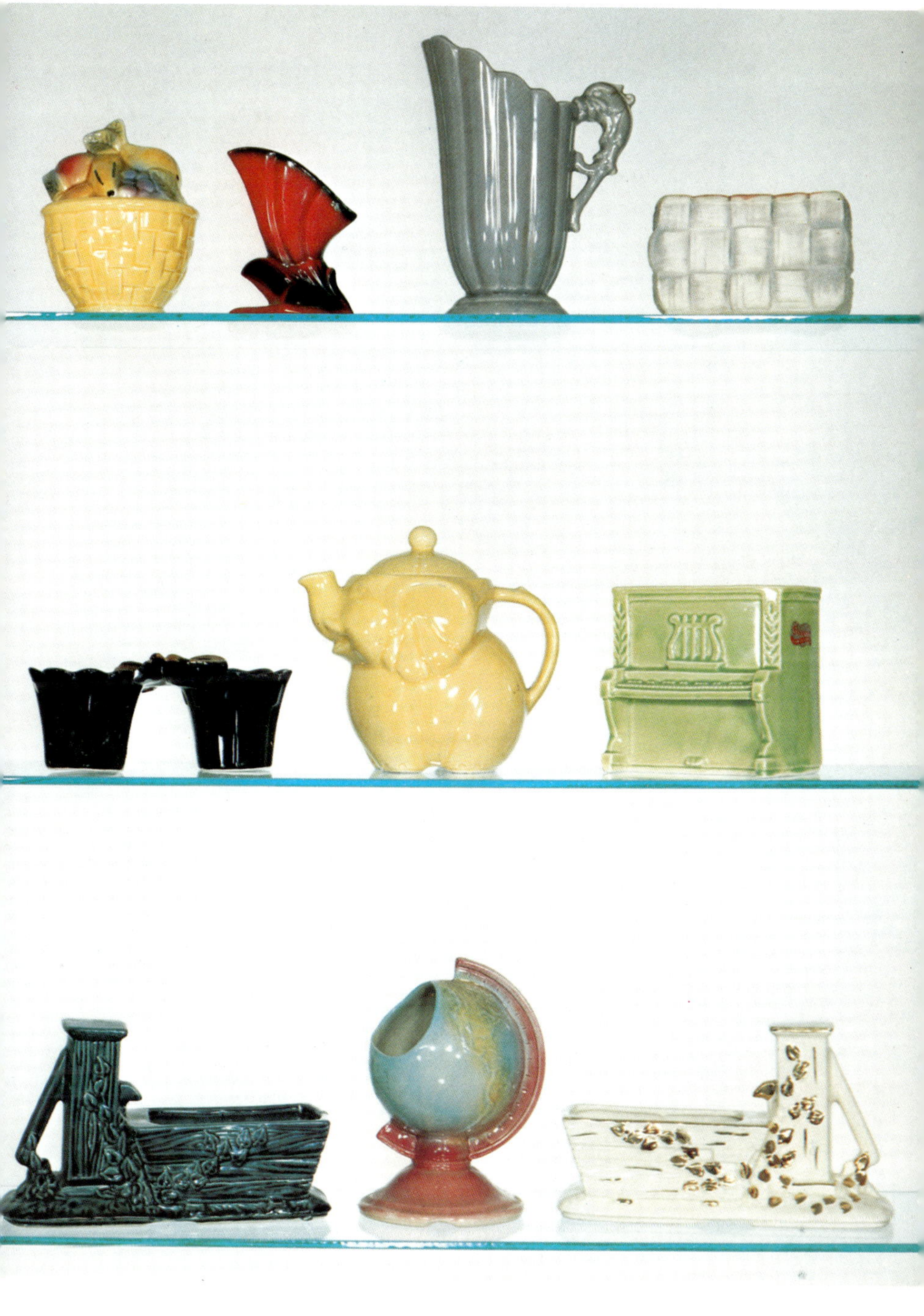

PLATE 9

Top Row -1. Figural Oriental man planter, marked U.S.A. #617. 2. Bow Knot vase, marked U.S.A. #819. 3. Vase with heavy gold overglaze leaf design, marked Shawnee U.S.A. #805. 4. Figural clown flower pot holder, marked U.S.A. #619.

Middle Row - 1. Planter, marked U.S.A. #132. 2. Figural covered wagon planter, marked Shawnee U.S.A. #733. 3. Figural Grist mill planter, marked Shawnee U.S.A. #769.

Bottom Row - 1. Figural clock planter, marked U.S.A. #530. 2. Figural alarm clock planter, marked U.S.A. #1262. 3. Truck planter with separate trailer planter, marked U.S.A. #680, and Shawnee U.S.A. #681. 4. Figural trolley planter, marked U.S.A.

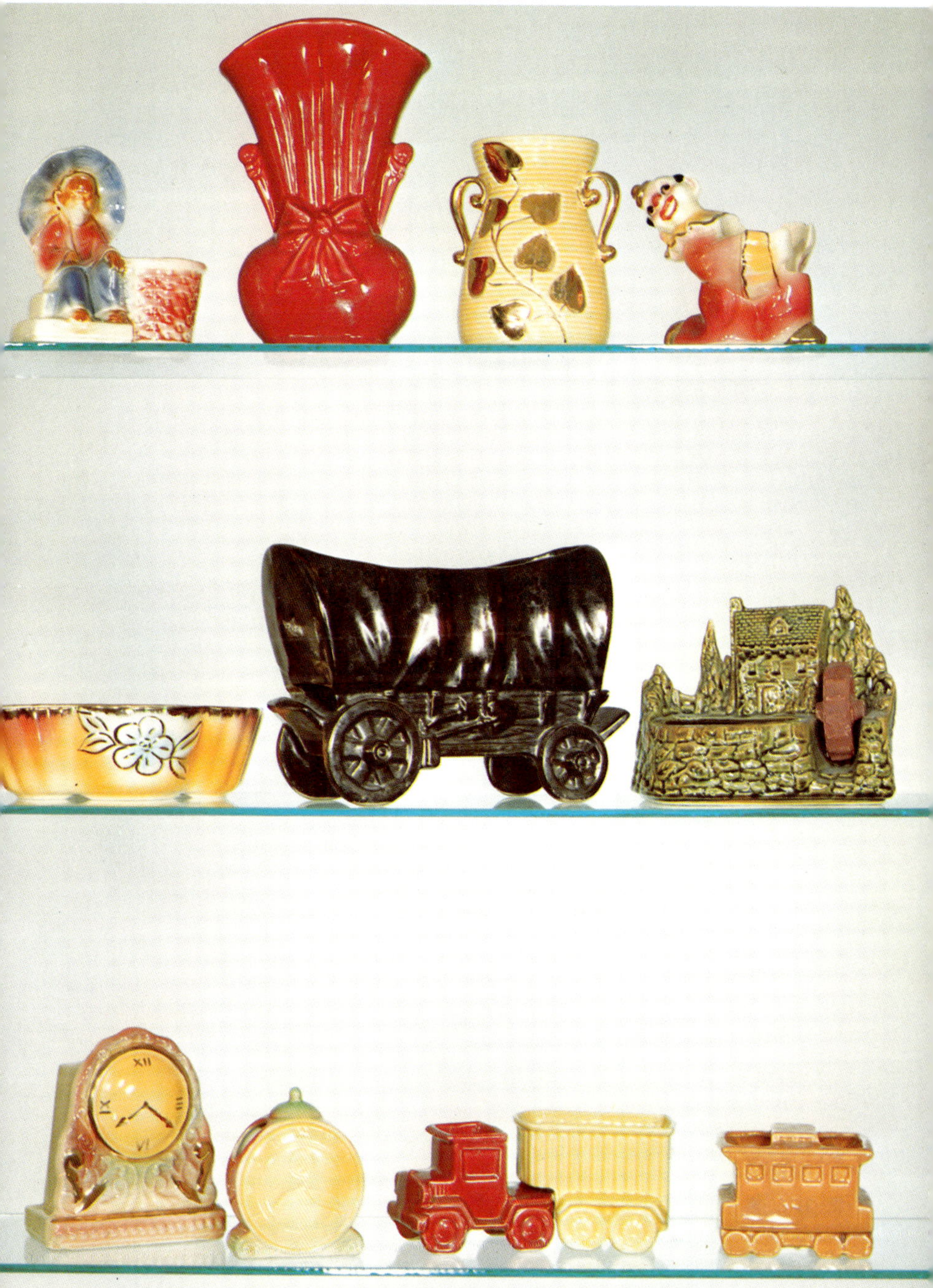

PLATE 10

Top Row - 1. Pair baby shoes planter, marked U.S.A. 2. Figural elf shoe planter, marked Shawnee U.S.A.#765. 3. Square white planter, marked Shawnee U.S.A. #450. 4. Square green planter, marked Shawnee U.S.A. #767.

Middle Row - 1. Planter with attached liner, marked Shawnee U.S.A. #463. 2. Small tray, marked U.S.A. #352. 3. Planter wine with stripes, marked U.S.A. #3005. 4. Planter with attached liner, marked Shawnee U.S.A. #410.

Bottom Row - 1. Planter with attached liner, marked U.S.A. #454. 2. Large footed planter, marked Shawnee U.S.A. #163. 3. Large quilted round planter marked Shawnee U.S.A. #457.

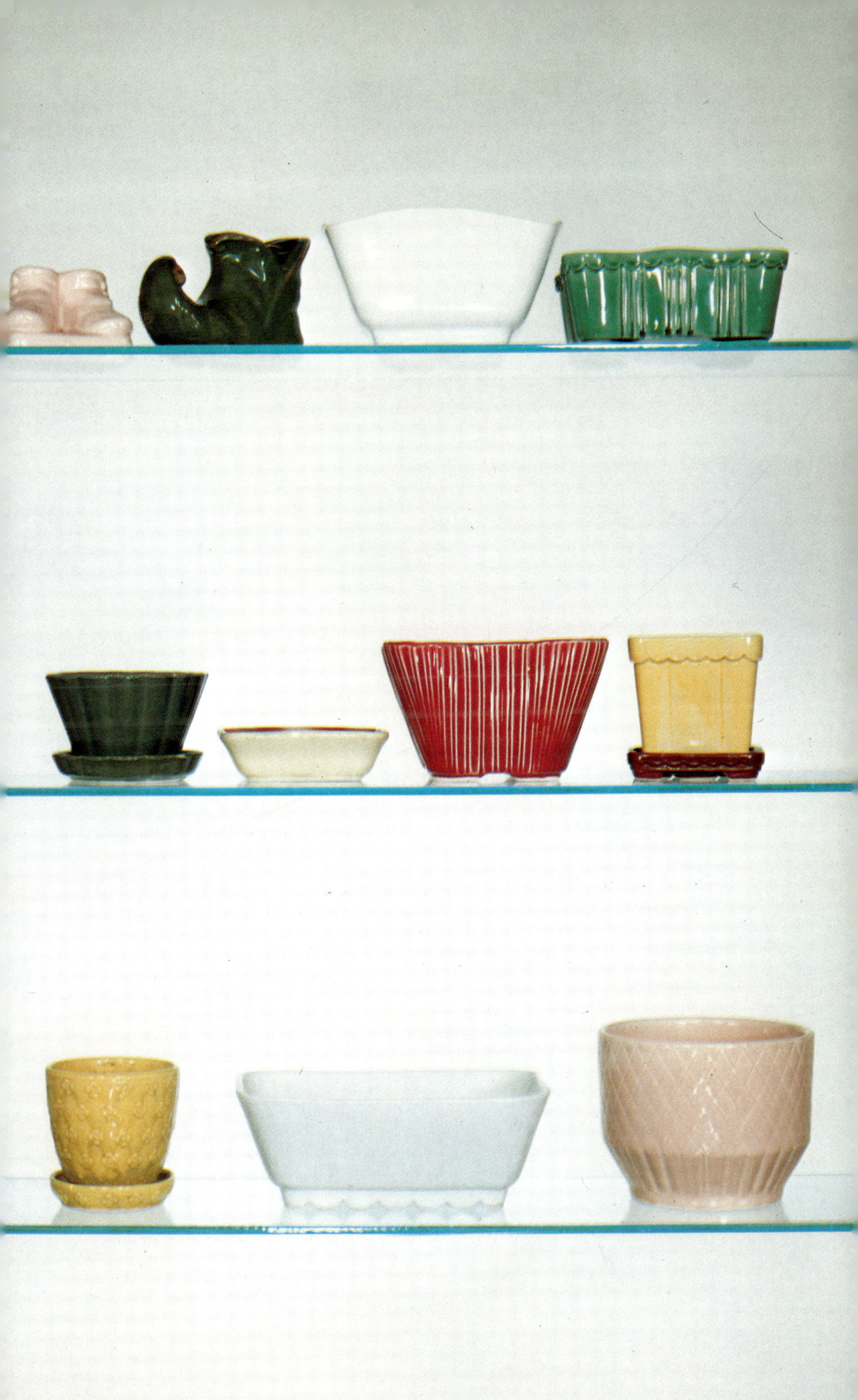

PLATE 11

Top Row - 1. Planter with attached liner 4″ green, marked Shawnee U.S.A. #454. 2. Planter with attached liner 2½″ same as #1, marked Shawnee U.S.A. #452. 3. Seashell planter blue, marked Shawnee U.S.A. #154. 4. Seashell planter wine, marked Shawnee U.S.A. #154. This item was made in several colors.

Middle Row - 1. Planter with attached liner 4″, marked Shawnee U.S.A. #454. 2. Planter quilted pink 4″, marked Shawnee U.S.A. #455. 3. Planter with attached liner, marked Shawnee U.S.A. #485. 4. Planter with attached liner, marked Shawnee U.S.A. #534.

Bottom Row - 1. Planter with leaf design, marked Shawnee U.S.A. #465. 2. Planter with attached tray, marked Shawnee U.S.A. #484. 3. Planter with attached tray 5″, marked Shawnee U.S.A. #495. 4. Planter with attached tray 3″, marked Shawnee U.S.A. #533.

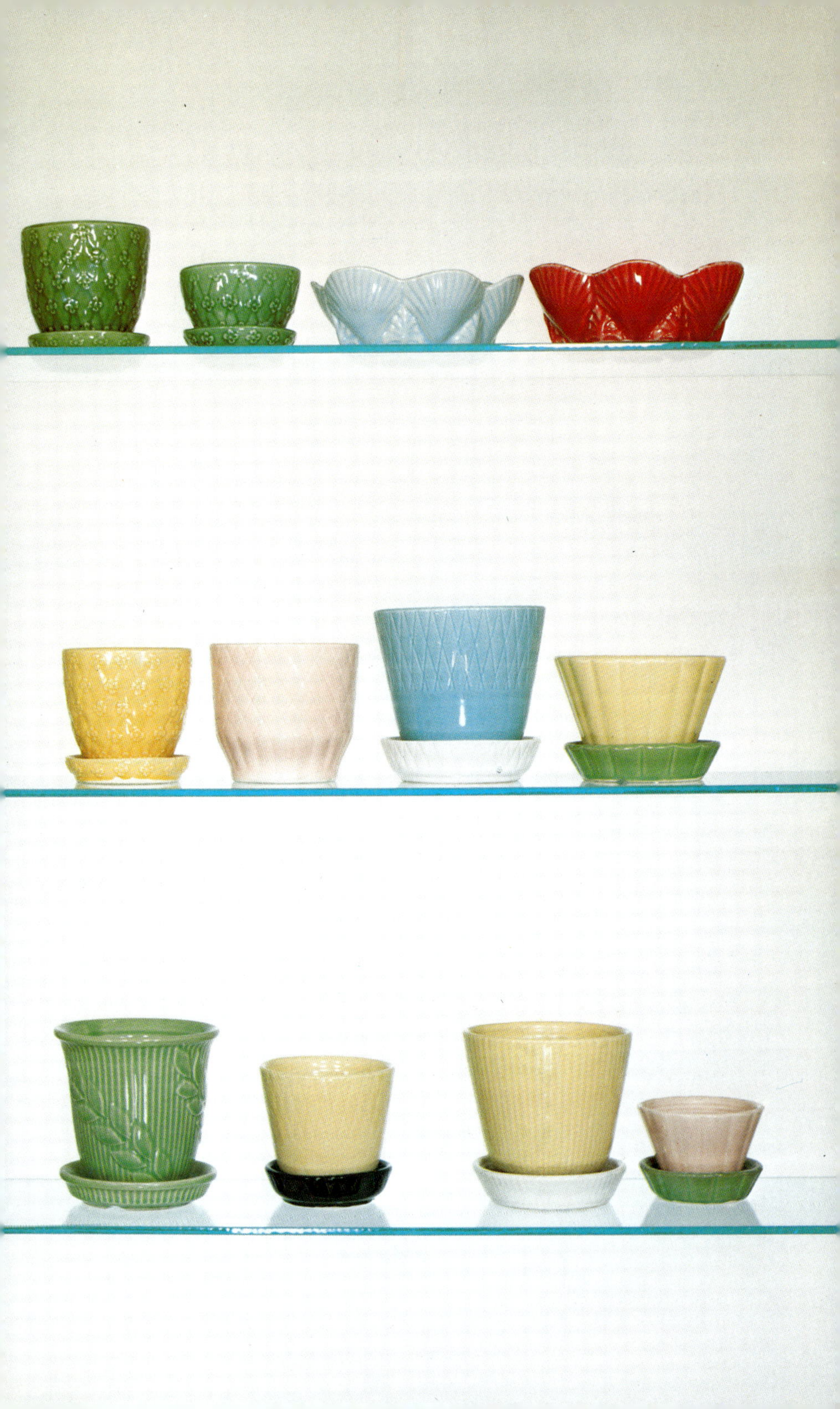

PLATE 12

Top Row - 1. Planter with attached liner 3", marked Shawnee U.S.A. 2. Cameo line ruffled vase, grey, marked Shawnee U.S.A. #2502. 3. Cameo line planter, blue, marked Shawnee U.S.A. #2505. 4. Elegance line footed planter, orange with original black and gold sticker, marked Shawnee U.S.A. #1404.

Middle Row - 1. Figural windmill planter, marked Shawnee U.S.A. #715. 2. Footed orange planter, marked U.S.A. #131. 3. Cameo line lilac planter bowl, marked Shawnee U.S.A. #2500.

Bottom Row - 1. African violet planter, yellow, marked U.S.A. #8001. 2. Oak leaf ashtray, marked U.S.A. #350. 3. Figural cat inkwell, marked U.S.A. #673. 4. Kenwood line ashtray and coaster, marked Shawnee U.S.A. #411. 5. African violet planter, pink, marked U.S.A. #8001.

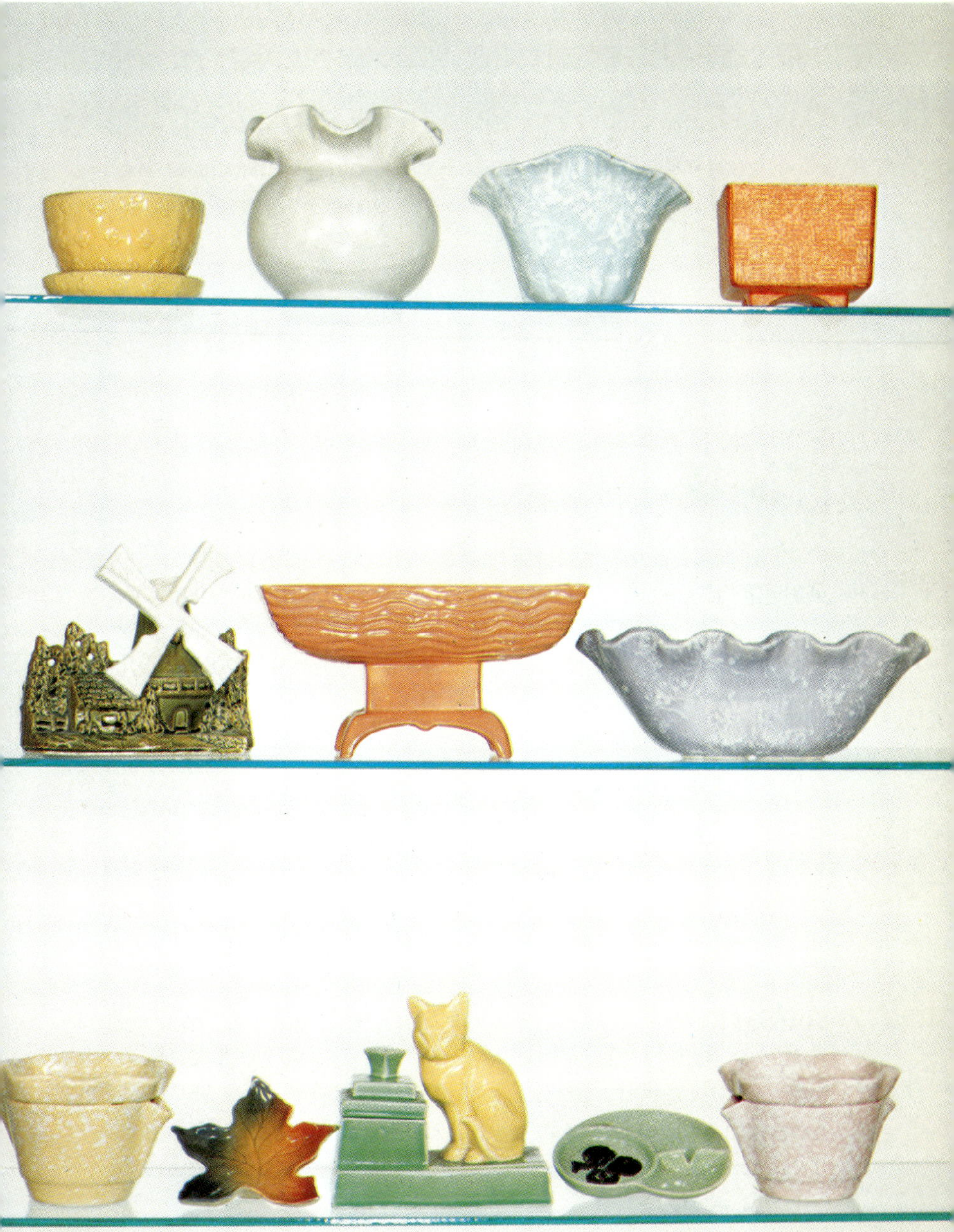

PLATE 13

Top Row - 1. Liana line planter, yellow, marked Shawnee U.S.A. #1007. 2. Touche line pillow vase, marked Shawnee U.S.A. #1012. 3. Touche line planter, marked U.S.A. #1004. 4. Touche line planter, marked Shawnee U.S.A. #1004.

Middle Row - 1. Touche line footed planter, marked Shawnee U.S.A. #1025. 2. Touche pillow vase, marked Shawnee U.S.A. #1026. 3. Liana line planter, marked Shawnee U.S.A. #1008. 4. Touche line planter, marked Shawnee U.S.A. #1011.

Bottom Row - 1. Bow Knot planter, marked U.S.A. 2. Tiara line candlestick, marked Shawnee U.S.A. 3. Tiara line console bowl, marked Shawnee U.S.A. #3504. 4. Tiara line candlestick, marked Shawnee U.S.A. 5. Navy blue small planter, marked U.S.A.

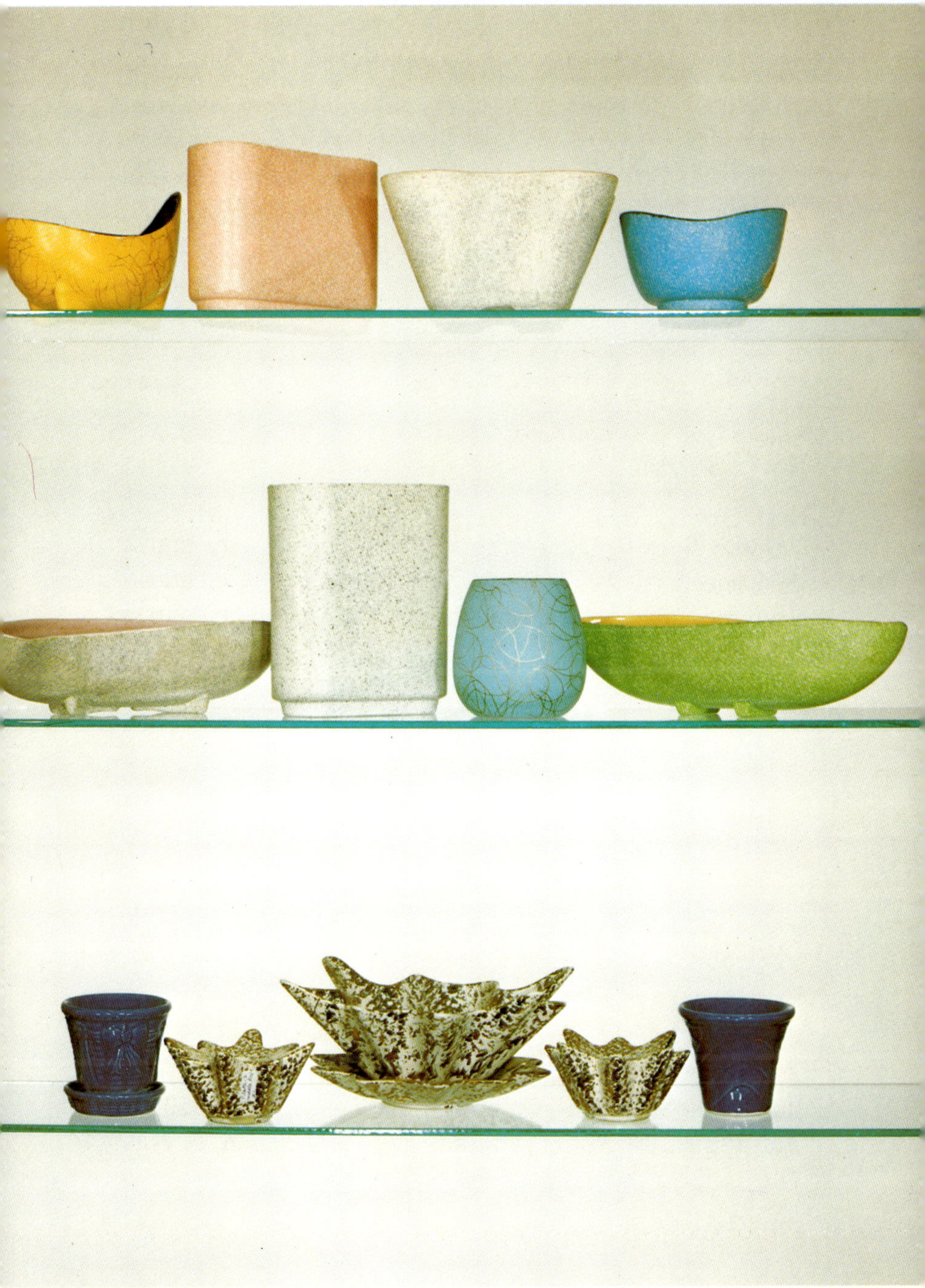

PLATE 14

Top Row - 1. Pair candle holders, marked U.S.A. #1386. 2. Woodtone planter, marked Shawnee U.S.A. #1201. 3. Tulip embossed planter, marked U.S.A.

Second Row - 1. Elegance line tall bud vase, marked Shawnee U.S.A. #1402. 2. High gloss vase, marked Shawnee U.S.A. #880. This vase was made in several colors. 3. High gloss vase, marked Shawnee U.S.A. #880. 4 Cameo line vase, marked Shawnee U.S.A. #2513.

Third Row - 1. Elegance line vase, marked Shawnee U.S.A. #1408. 2. Woodtone ashtray, marked U.S.A. #1014. 3. Vase, brown high gloss wood grain, marked Shawnee U.S.A. #868.

Bottom Row - 1. Kenwood Sun Dial line, covered casserole, marked Shawnee U.S.A. 2. Kenwood line ashtray, marked Kenwood U.S.A #2125.

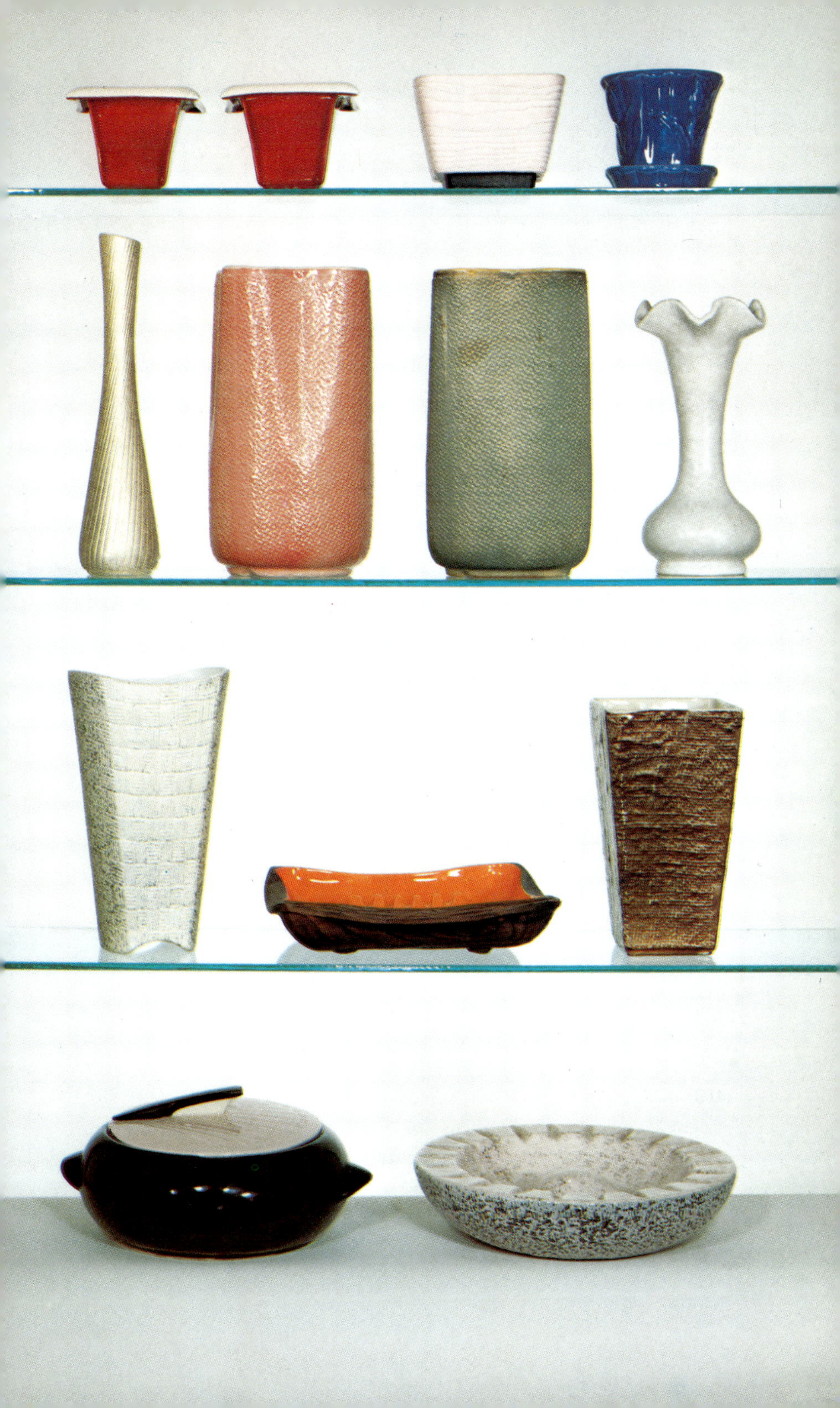

PLATE 15

Top Row - 1. Pineapple vase, marked Shawnee U.S.A. #839. 2. Large vase, pink with spillover black enamel, marked U.S.A. #2146. 3. Cameo line tall bud vase, marked Shawnee U.S.A. #2511.

Middle Row - 1. Elegance line orange planter, marked Shawnee U.S.A. #1006. 2. Swirl vase, green with ruffled top, marked U.S.A. #606. 3. Vase, woodgrain dull finish, marked Shawnee U.S.A. #879. 4. Swirl vase, white with ruffled top, marked U.S.A.#606. 5. Elegance line gourd planter, marked Shawnee U.S.A. #1007.

Bottom Row - 1. Touche line vase, marked Shawnee U.S.A. #1013. 2. Touche footed flat sided planter, marked Shawnee U.S.A. #1024. 3. Miniature vase, marked U.S.A. #1135. 4. Cameo line ruffled bowl, marked Shawnee U.S.A. #2507.

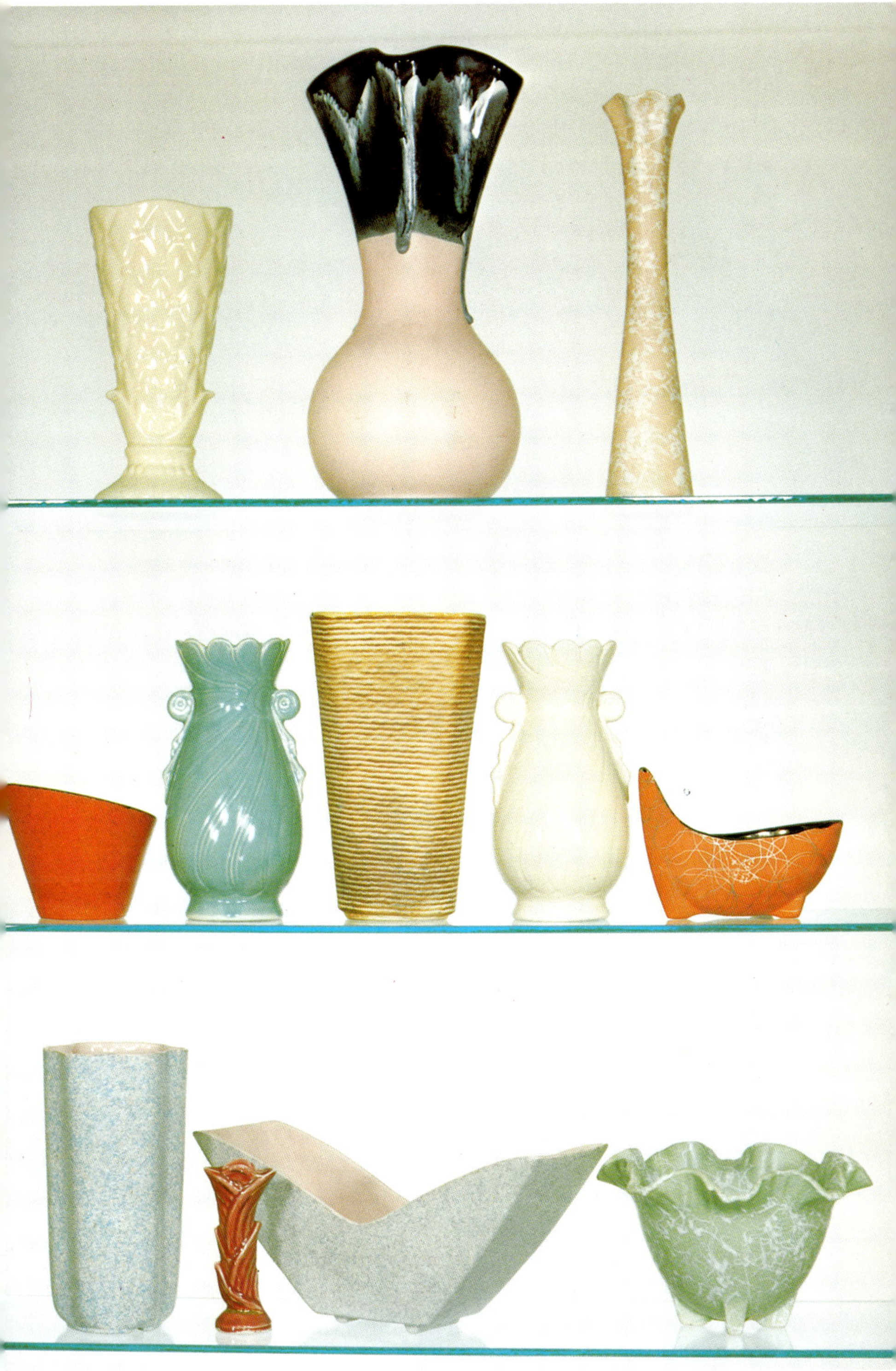

PLATE 16

Top Row - 1. Figural Dutch girl cookie jar, marked U.S.A. 2. Figural Dutch boy cookie jar, marked U.S.A. 3. Figural farmer pig cookie jar, marked U.S.A.

Middle Row - 1. Puss n Boots lady cookie jar, marked Patented Puss N Boots U.S.A. 2. Puss N Boots lady cookie jar, marked Patented U.S.A. 3. Dutch girl cookie jar, marked U.S.A.

Bottom Row - 1. Smiley pig combination cookie jar and bank, marked Patent Smiley #60. Shawnee U.S.A. 2. Winnie pig combination cookie jar and bank, marked Shawnee U.S.A. #61. Patent Winnie. 3. Lady pig cookie jar, marked U.S.A.

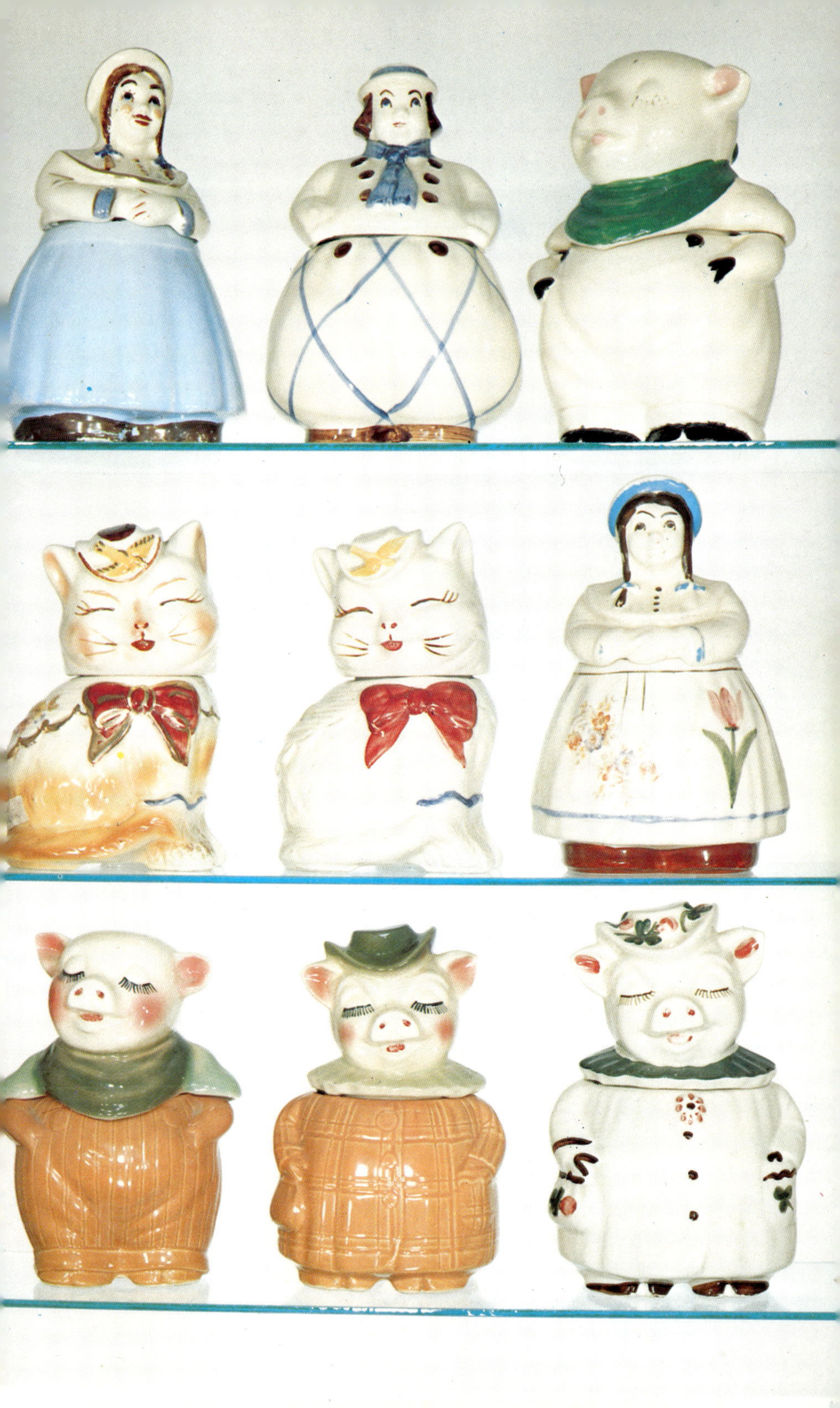

PLATE 17

Top Row - 1. Pair figural puppy dog shakers. 2. Basket of fruit cookie jar, marked Shawnee U.S.A. #84. 3. Pair figural flower pot shakers, no mark except paper label.

Middle Row - 1. Pair milk pail shakers, marked with paper label. 2. Dutch girl cookie jar, marked Great Northern U.S.A. #1026. This cookie jar was manufactured by the Great Northern for Merchandise Mart in Chicago, from a Shawnee mold. 3. Pair figural elephant shakers, marked with a paper label.

Bottom Row - 1. Pair Mugsey figural shakers, 2. Mugsey dog cookie jar, marked U.S.A. 3. Pair figural owl shakers with grey eyes, marked U.S.A. 4. Owl cookie jar, marked U.S.A. 5. Pair figural owl shakers with green eyes, marked U.S.A.

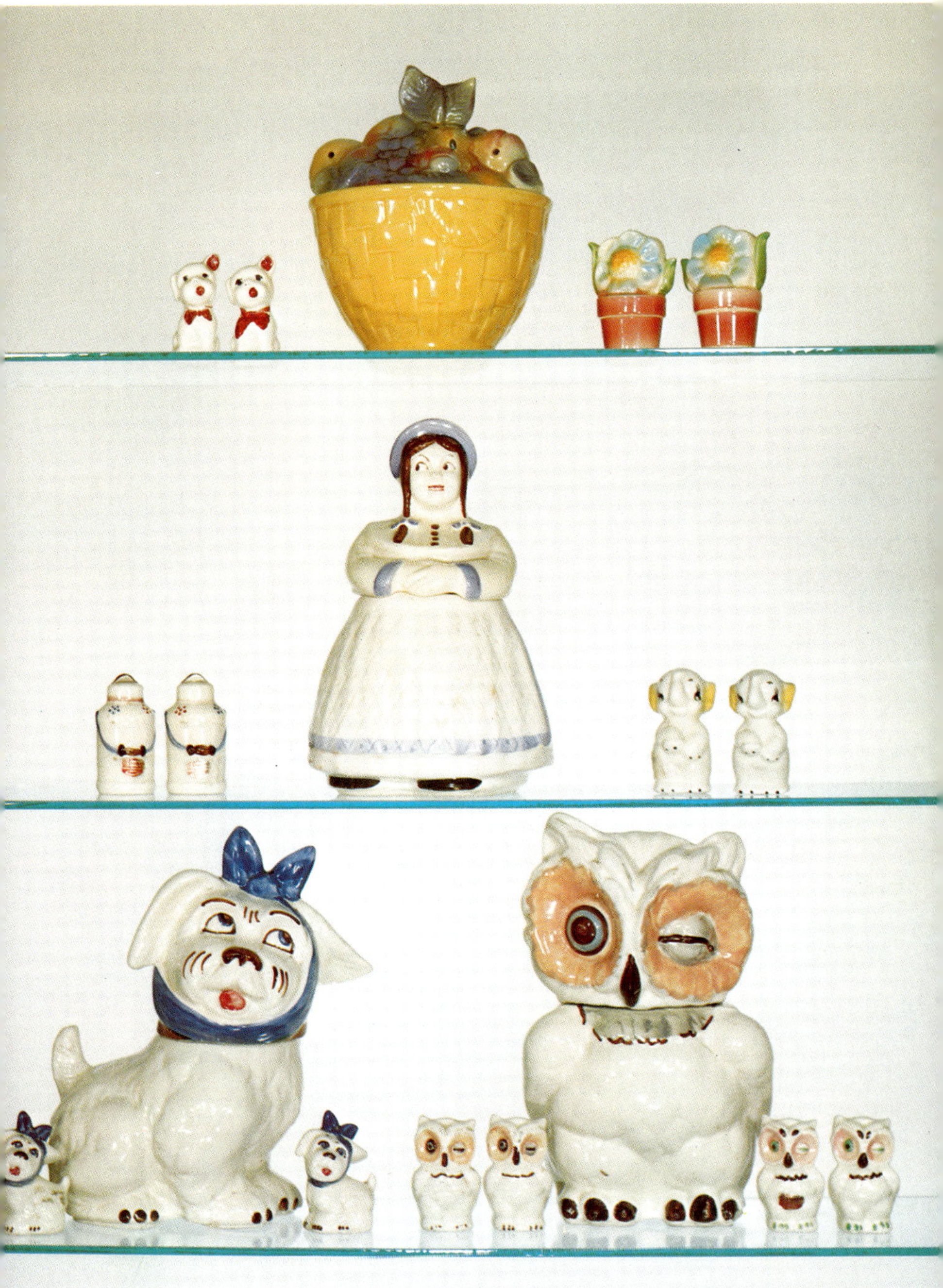

PLATE 18

Top Row - 1. Pair figural boy pig shakers. 2. Pair figural pig shakers. 3. Pair figural Winnie and boy pig shakers.

Second Row - 1. Pair water can shakers. 2. Pair water can shakers, different pattern. 3. Set of three farmer pig shakers.

Third Row - 1. Pair Winnie shakers. 2. Pair sailor boy shakers. 3. Little Bo Peep pair shakers.

Bottom Row -1. Pair elephant shakers with pink ears. 2. Pair elephant shakers with green ears. 3. Puss n Boots shakers.

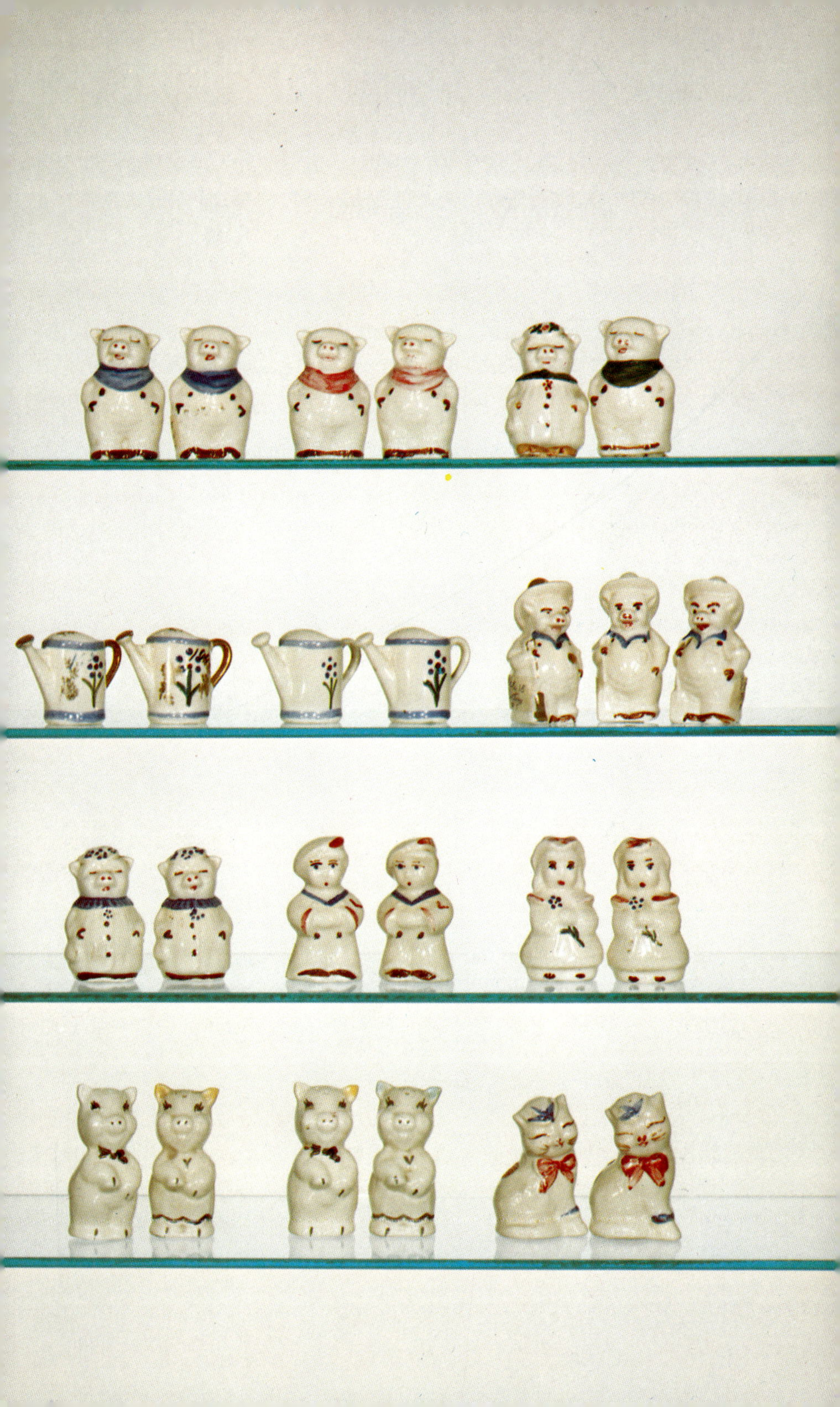

PLATE 19

Top Row - Pair 5″ Winnie and farmer pig shakers. 2. Pair 5″ Farmer and Winnie pig shakers, in other colors. 3. Pair 5″ mugsey dog shakers.

Middle Row - 1. Figural Puss N Boots cream pitcher, marked Shawnee U.S.A. #85. 2. Figural elephant cream pitcher, marked Patented U.S.A. 3. Figural pig cream pitcher, marked Patented Smiley U.S.A. 4. Figural Puss N Boots cream pitcher, marked Patented Puss N Boots U.S.A.

Bottom Row - 1. Pair 5″ figural pig shakers. 2. Bo Peep milk pitcher 8″, marked Bo Peep U.S.A. 3. Bo Peep milk pitcher, marked Patented Bo Peep U.S.A. 4. Pair 5″ Dutch boy and girl shakers.

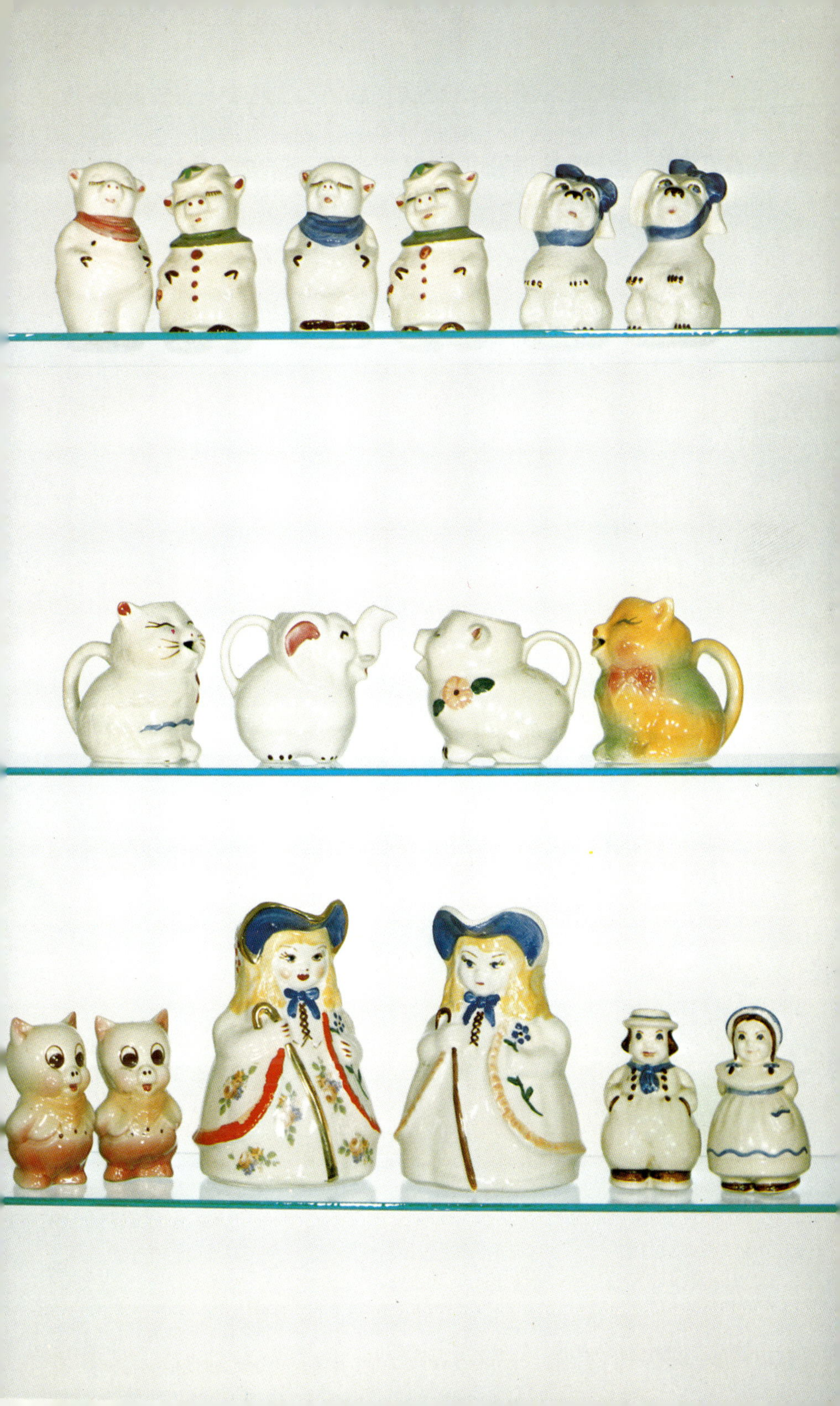

PLATE 20

Top Row - 1. Figural Granny Ann teapot, green, marked Patented Granny Ann U.S.A. 2. figural Granny Ann teapot, blue, marked U.S.A.

Second Row - 1. Figural Tom Tom the Pipers Son teapot, marked Patented U.S.A. #44. Has a lot of gold over glaze. 2. Figural Tom Tom the Pipers Son teapot, marked same as #1. 3. Figural Tom Tom the Pipers Son teapot, marked U.S.A. This one is trimmed in brown. Also seen in other colors.

Third Row - 1. Figural sailor boy milk pitcher 7½", marked Shawnee U.S.A. #46. 2. Figural Bo Peep milk pitcher 7½", marked Shawnee U.S.A. #47. 3. Figural rooster planter, marked Shawnee U.S.A. #503. 4. Figural cat playing horn planter, marked Shawnee U.S.A. #729.

Bottom Row - 1. Figural Smiley pig two quart water jug, marked Patented Smiley U.S.A. This has heavy gold over glaze. 2. Figural Smiley two quart water jug, but no gold trim. Marked Smiley U.S.A. 3. Figural chicken water jug, marked Charlicleer, U.S.A.

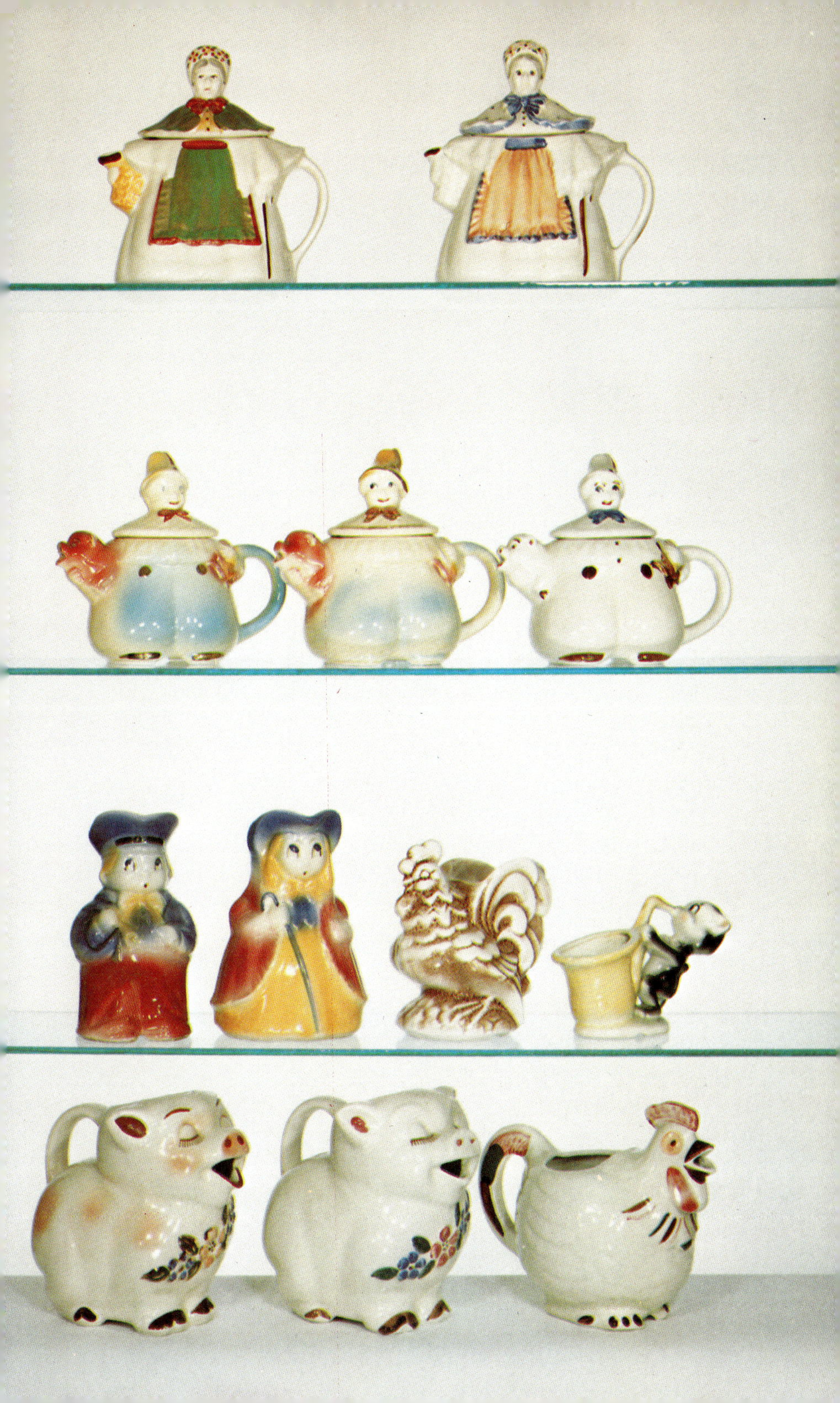

PLATE 21. Lamps

Top Row - 1. Oriental lady planter, no mark. 2. Pair 12″ grape encrusted lamps, marked with paper label only. 3. Oriental man planter, no mark.

Middle Row - 1. Pair of lamps floral hand painted, marked with paper label only. 2. Pair of lamps, Oriental design, marked with paper label only.

Bottom Row - 1. Pair of lamps with flowers in high relief, marked with paper label only. 2. Pair lamps, urn shaped. Marked with paper label only.

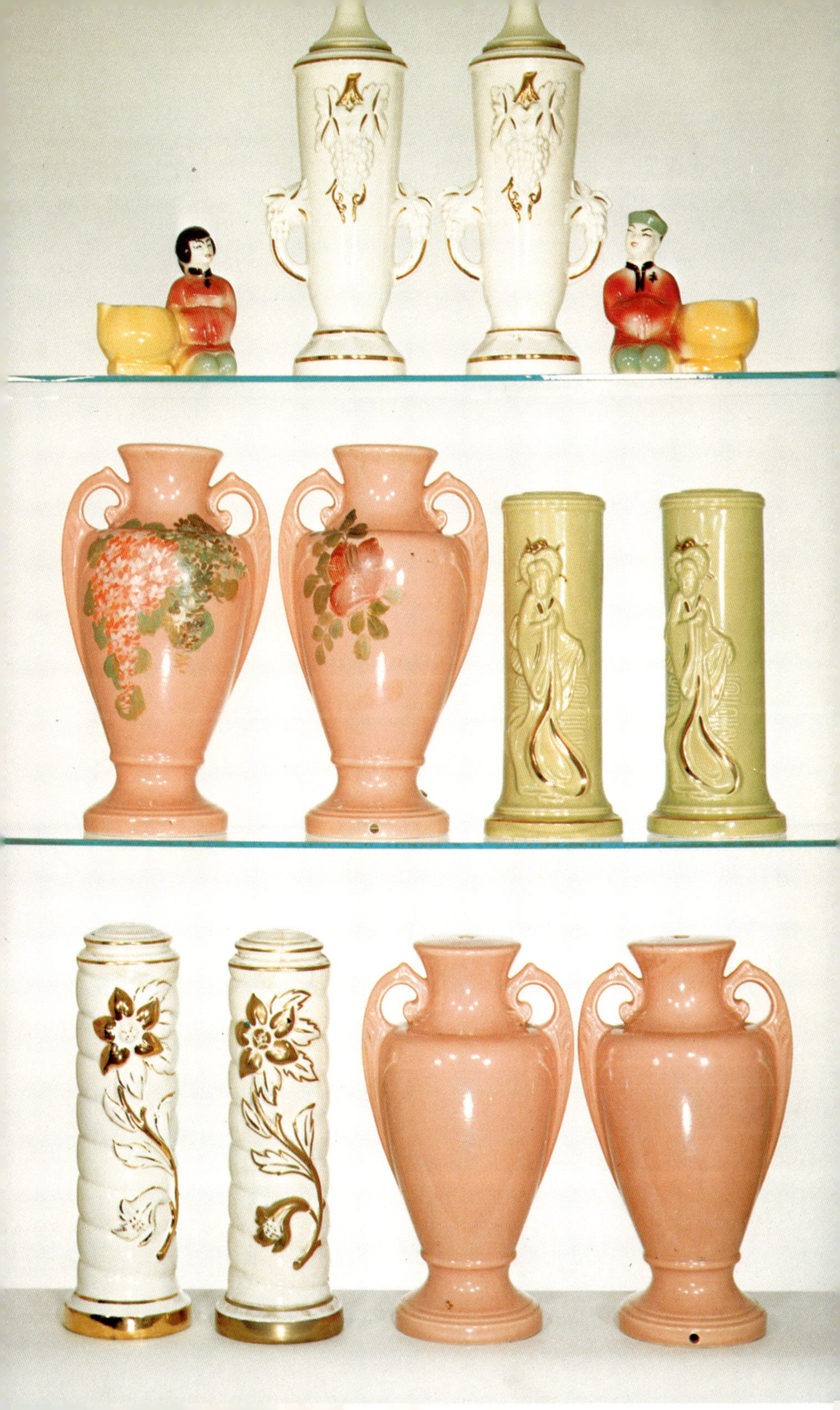

PLATE 22

Top Row - 1. Flying goose planter, marked Shawnee U.S.A. #820. 2. Oriental figure planter, marked U.S.A. #574. 3. Basket, made by the Shawnee company for Rum Rill Pottery company, marked Rum Rill, #348.

Second Row - 1. Kenwood line planter, marked Shawnee U.S.A. #1608. 2. Touche line planter, marked Shawnee U.S.A. #1406. Planter, marked U.S.A. #181.

Third Row - 1. Bud vase, made for Rum Rill, marked Rum Rill. 2. Woodtone vase, marked Shawnee U.S.A. #1208. 3. Woodtone vase, marked Shawnee U.S.A. #1212.

Bottom Row - 1. Vase, made for the Rum Rill Pottery company, marked Rum Rill #353. 2. Cameo line planter, marked Shawnee U.S.A. #2506. 3. Art line vase, made for the RUM RILL Pottery company, marked RUM RILL #505.

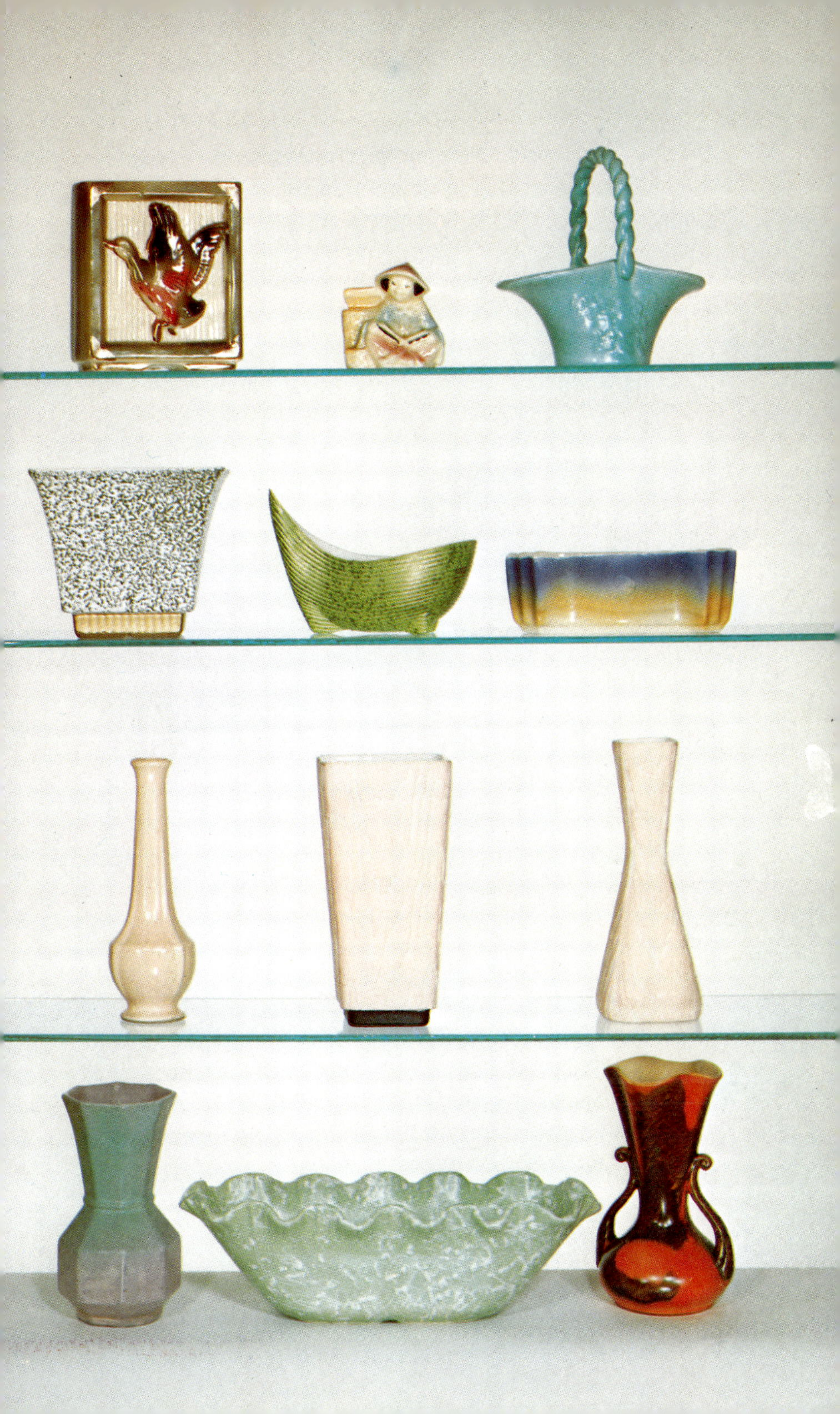

PLATE 23 Rum Rill Pottery

This page along with a few pieces from the preceding page, are Shawnee Pottery manufactured, and were made for the Rum Rill Pottery Company. They were made in the late 1930's and early pre-war 1940's. Prior to this, Rum Rill pottery was made by the Red Wing Pottery company in Red Wing Minnesota.

Top Row - 1. Figural duck. 2. Pair jug candleholders, marked 1500 and applied Rum Rill labels. The candles are mercury glass. 3. Figural bird, marked #604.

Middle Row - 1. Figural penquin. 2. Pair figural pouter pigeons, marked #359. 3. Figural blue duck. 4. Figural dove, marked with Rum Rill label. 5. Pair of shell candleholders, marked #1911.

Bottom Row - 1. Figural deer, marked #901. 2. Figural girl statue, marked 477. 3. Figural flying goose planter. 4. Pair of figural shell candleholders, marked #1911.

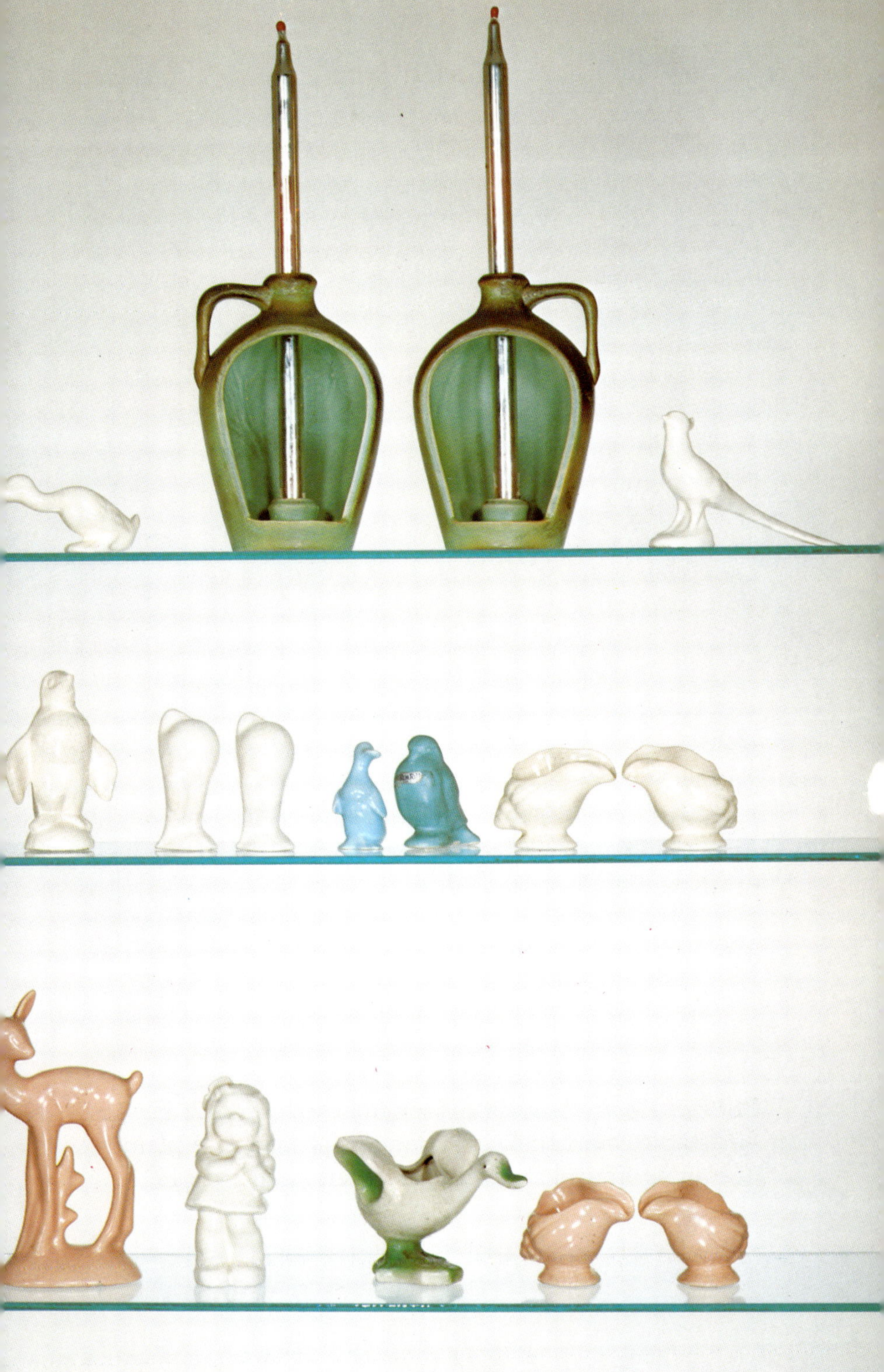

The current values in this book should be used only as a guide. They are not intended to set prices, which vary from one section of the country to another. Auction prices as well as dealer prices vary greatly and are affected by condition as well as demand. Neither the Author nor the Publisher assumes responsibility for any losses that might be incurred as a result of consulting this guide.

PLATE 1

Top Row	- 1. $10.00	2. $10.00	3. $10.00	4. $ 9.00
Middle Row	- 1. $ 9.00	2. $ 6.00	3. $ 5.00	4. $ 7.00
Bottom Row	- 1. $ 7.00	2. $ 7.00	3. $ 7.00	4. $ 9.00

PLATE 2

Top Row	- 1. $24.00	2. $24.00	3. $ 7.00	4. $ 6.00
Middle Row	- 1. $ 6.00	2. $ 6.00	3. $ 7.00	4. $ 7.00
Bottom Row	- 1. $ 9.00	2. $ 7.00	3. $ 7.00	4. $ 6.00

PLATE 3

Top Row	- 1. $ 6.00	2. $ 6.00	3. $ 7.00	4. $10.00
	5. $ 9.00			
Middle Row	- 1. $ 5.00	2. $ 6.00	3. $10.00	4. $11.00
Bottom Row	- 1. $14.00 pr.	2. $ 5.00	3. $ 6.00	4. $ 6.00

PLATE 4

Top Row	- 1. $10.50	2. $10.50	3. $10.50	4. $ 9.00
Middle Row	- 1. $ 9.00	2. $ 9.00	3. $10.00	4. $ 9.00
Bottom Row	- 1. $ 7.00	2. $ 9.00	3. $10.00	4. $ 7.00

PLATE 5

Top Row	- 1. $ 7.00 pr.	2. $ 7.00 pr.	3. $ 7.00 pr.	4. $12.00 pr.
Middle Row	- 1. $ 7.00	2. $ 9.00	3. $ 9.00	4. $ 6.00
Bottom Row	- 1. $ 9.00	2. $ 6.00	3. $ 6.00	

PLATE 6

Top Row	- 1. $27.00	2. $22.00	3. $14.00	
Middle Row	- 1. $ 7.00	2. $10.50	3. $12.00	4. $ 5.00
	5. $ 9.00			
Bottom Row	- 1. $11.00	2. $18.00	3. $ 9.00	4. $ 6.00

PLATE 7

Top Row	- 1. $ 9.00	2. $ 6.00	3. $10.00
Middle Row	- 1. $ 6.00	2. $22.00	3. $ 6.00
Bottom Row	- 1. $ 6.00	2. $ 7.00	3. $10.00

PLATE 8

Top Row	- 1. $10.00	2. $10.00	3. $12.00	4. $ 6.00	
Middle Row	- 1. $11.00	2. $10.50	3. $ 9.00		
Bottom Row	- 1. $10.00	2. $10.00	3. $12.00		

PLATE 9

Top Row	- 1. $ 7.00	2. $ 7.00	3. $10.50	4. $ 9.00	
Middle Row	- 1. $ 6.00	2. $14.00	3. $10.50		
Bottom Row	- 1. $ 9.00	2. $ 7.00	3. $ 6.00	4. $ 5.00	5. $ 6.00

PLATE 10

Top Row	- 1. $ 5.00	2. $ 9.00	3. $ 6.00	4. $ 6.00
Middle Row	- 1. $ 5.50	2. $ 5.00	3. $ 5.00	4. $ 6.00
Bottom Row	- 1. $ 5.50	2. $ 6.00	3. $ 7.00	

PLATE 11

Top Row	- 1. $ 6.00	2. $ 5.00	3. $ 6.00	4. $ 6.00
Middle Row	- 1. $ 6.00	2. $ 6.00	3. $ 6.00	4. $ 6.00
Bottom Row	- 1. $ 6.00	2. $ 5.00	3. $ 6.00	4. $ 5.00

PLATE 12

Top Row	- 1. $ 5.00	2. $ 7.00	3. $ 7.00	4. $ 7.00	
Middle Row	- 1. $11.00	2. $ 6.00	3. $ 9.00		
Bottom Row	- 1. $ 6.00	2. $ 6.00	3. $10.00	4. $ 5.00	5. $ 6.00

PLATE 13

Top Row	- 1. $ 6.00	2. $ 6.00	3. $ 6.00	4. $ 6.00
Middle Row	- 1. $ 7.00	2. $ 7.00	3. $ 6.00	4. $ 7.00
Bottom Row	- 1. $ 5.00	2. $12.00 pr.	3. $12.00	4. $ 5.00

PLATE 14

Top Row	- 1. $10.00 pr.	2. $ 6.00	3. $ 5.00	
Second Row	- 1. $10.00	2. $10.00	3. $10.00	4. $ 9.00
Third Row	- 1. $ 9.00	2. $ 9.00	3. $ 9.00	
Bottom Row	- 1. $18.00	2. $10.00		

PLATE 15

Top Row	- 1. $10.00	2. $12.00	3. $10.00		
Middle Row	- 1. $ 6.00	2. $ 7.00	3. $ 9.00	4. $ 7.00	5. $ 7.00
Bottom Row	- 1. $ 9.00	2. $ 5.00	3. $10.00	4. $ 9.00	

PLATE 16

Top Row	- 1. $22.00	2. $22.00	3. $24.00
Middle Row	- 1. $26.00	2. $26.00	3. $22.00
Bottom Row	- 1. $30.00	2. $30.00	3. $30.00

PLATE 17

Top Row	- 1. $ 6.00	2. $22.00	3. $ 9.00 pr.	
Middle Row	- 1. $ 7.00 pr.	2. $18.00	3. $ 7.00 pr.	
Bottom Row	- 1. $10.00 pr.	2. $26.00	3. $10.00 pr.	4. $26.00
	5. $10.00 pr.			

PLATE 18

Top Row	- 1. $10.00 pr.	2. $10.00 pr.	3. $11.00 pr.
Second Row	- 1. $ 9.00 pr.	2. $ 9.00 pr.	3. $ 5.00 ea.
Third Row	- 1. $11.00 pr.	2. $10.50 pr.	3. $11.00 pr.
Bottom Row	- 1. $ 9.00 pr.	2. $ 9.00 pr.	3. $11.00 pr.

PLATE 19

Top Row	- 1. $14.00 pr.	2. $14.00 pr.	3. $14.00 pr.	4. $14.00 pr.
Middle Row	- 1. $11.00	2. $11.00	3. $11.00	4. $11.00
Bottom Row	- 1. $12.00 pr.	2. $18.00	3. $18.00	4. $12.00 pr.

PLATE 20

Top Row	- 1. $24.00	2. $24.00		
Second Row	- 1. $24.00	2. $24.00	3. $24.00	
Third Row	- 1. $14.00	2. $14.00	3. $10.00	4. $ 9.00
Bottom Row	- 1. $22.00	2. $22.00	3. $18.00	

PLATE 21

Top Row	- 1. $ 7.00	2. $42.00 pr.	3. $ 7.00
Middle Row	- 1. $42.00 pr.	2. $36.00 pr.	
Bottom Row	- 1. $36.00 pr.	2. $38.00 pr.	

PLATE 22

Top Row	- 1. $10.50	2. $ 6.00	3. $27.00
Second Row	- 1. $ 9.00	2. $ 9.00	3. $ 6.00
Third Row	- 1. $18.00	2. $10.00	3. $ 9.00
Bottom Row	- 1. $18.00	2. $11.00	3. $42.00

PLATE 23

Top Row	- 1. $ 6.00	2. $24.00 pr.	3. $ 6.00	
Middle Row	- 1. $ 6.00	2. $ 6.00	3. $ 6.00	4. $ 6.00
	5. $10.00	6. $ 9.00		
Bottom Row	- 1. $ 7.00	2. $ 7.00	3. $ 7.00	4. $ 9.00 pr.

LINE NUMBERS

The following numbers are in sequence with the line designs that were manufactured by the Shawnee Pottery Company while they were in operation. Many of the pieces are marked with a number only, while some are marked with a number and the letters, U.S.A. This list will give the collector an idea of what numbers are found on the various pieces made.

1. 0 to #154, mostly small planters with animals and people.
2. #401 to 500, general planters
3. #501 to 896, remainder of people and animal planters.
4. #900 to 935, Lobster line. This is the Kenwood Ceramics Division of Shawnee.
5. #945 to 991, Kenwood line.
6. #994 to 998, Lobster line on the Sundial base.
7. #1000 to 2014, newer Kenwood line.
8. #2015 to 2032, Kenwood line animal planters.
9. #1003 to 1028, Liana line by Shawnee.
10. #3000 Kashani line by Kenwood.
11. #1500 Medallion by Kenwood.
12. #2100 Confetti by Kenwood
13. #1600 Diora by Shawnee.
14. #1800 Chantilly by Shawnee.
15. #1900 Petit Point by Shawnee.
16. #1400 Elegance by Shawnee.
17. #1700 Fern Ware by Shawnee.
18. #2000 Accent by Shawnee. (ashtrays).
19. #2500 Cameo by Shawnee.
20. #1900 Cherie by Shawnee, (same as Petit Point).
21. #1000's Touche by Shawnee (same as Liana).